To:

_____

From:

_____

Date:

_____

INTERNATIONAL

THE Family

THE Family

RESTORING THE MORAL
STRUCTURE OF THE FAMILY

GUILLERMO MALDONADO

OUR VISION

The objective of our mission is to spiritually feed God's people through preaching, teaching and the written word as we take the Word of God everywhere it is needed.

The Family: Restoring the family values

ISBN: 1-59272-087-0

Second Edition 2005

Cover designed by:
GM International - Design Department

Interior Design by:
GM International

Category:
"The Family"

Published by:
GM International
13651 SW 143 Ct., #101
Miami, FL 33186
(305) 233-3325 Fax (305) 233-3328

Printed by:
GM International

Printed in Colombia

Dedication

I dedicate this book to my Lord; I owe Him everything that I am. Also, I dedicate the words written in this book to every family, Christian or none Christian, and to every couple who plans to build a home and a family. In the name of Jesus, I declare your family blessed, even unto a thousand generations!

Acknowledgements

I want to take this opportunity to thank God for the blessing of such a beautiful family. They are my inspiration and unconditional support for this ministry.

Also, I want to express my deepest appreciation to every person that God has placed in my path and from whom I learn. Thank you for your prayers. To all the people that work behind the scenes and who made the publication of this book a reality, I thank you.

Index

Index

Introduction

According to Genesis 2.18, humanity was designed and created by God to live in fellowship. It has been proven beyond a shadow of a doubt that **the family** is the cell and fundamental foundation of society. The family unit is made up of a series of interpersonal relationships that grow continually.

Because **the family** is an irreplaceable institution, it should be defended at all costs. It is important to remember that the family, and its different dimensions, is the nucleus of society. The family unit is extremely important, especially because this is the place where the individual is conceived and born. It is necessary to look after this individual from his conception to make sure that he is loved, respected and appreciated as someone who is valuable and unique. He can not be imitated.

Chapter 1

Marriage is a Covenant

$\mathcal{W}$ hat we are about to share with you in this chapter is the foundation for building strong families. The rest of the study found in this book depends on the word "covenant". Fear of God is practically non-existent in our society today. Divorce is easy to achieve because people don't have a clear understanding of what the marriage covenant means. To understand this subject matter in a clear and easy to understand way, the word "covenant" needs to be defined:

A **covenant** is an agreement between two or more people who make a commitment to do something within the agreed specified stipulations. The agreement is achieved when there is a ratification of the document through the signatures of the parties involved. Through this contract, the parties involved are bound by the stipulations of the contract.

Now let us define the word "pact":

A **pact** includes a contract, but it is more than that. Relationships are needed to complete a pact, not only legal and formal documents. A personal relationship between the two parties signing an agreement is not needed for a contract to be legal. For example: I don't need to have a relationship with or be in the opposite party's good graces before signing a contract; the end result doesn't change, it is still a business transaction. On the other hand, in a pact, relationships are needed because the pact is based on the relationship.

In summation, a pact is the arrangement of a contract between two people, in which both are bound and committed by a relationship and a legal document. A pact is more than being restricted to someone by a document; it binds both parties through the relationship and the virtue that is given by God.

The Word of God teaches about three **pact** institutions, which were created by God, to fulfill His plans on earth. These are:

- The family
- The church
- The government

1. The family and marriage

God created marriage for three reasons and only one of these reasons has anything to do with man's happiness. The other two reasons are directly related to God's purpose and will.

- **To procreate.** Having children. God said to Adam, "Go and multiply."

  "27So God created man in His own image; in the image of God He created him; male and female He created them. 28Then God blessed them, and God said to them, "Be fruitful and multiply; fill the earth and subdue it; have dominion over the fish of the sea, over the birds of the air, and over every living thing that moves on the earth." Genesis 1.27, 28

The reason God said to married couples to have children was to exercise dominion and lordship over His creation, and not only to give birth to little kids so they can run around looking like their parents. Through these children, God's name will be known for an eternity, and His dominion and lordship will be established forever. Once our children grow up and move out of the house to become independent adults, they will make known the **name of God** throughout the nations.

- **To prevent man and woman from being alone.**

  This reason relates to man's happiness. God said, "I will give you a helper."

17

"18And the LORD God said, "It is not good that man should be alone; I will make him a helper comparable to him." Genesis 2.18

The reason God created woman was to complete what was missing in man. God is not going to provide a person identical to you; it is not necessary. The objective is for you to receive, through your spouse, what is missing or needed for you to fulfill the purpose of God for your life. The word "helper" means: one who protects; one who surrounds and covers.

Each spouse has a responsibility. God gives you a partner to fulfill His purpose for your life and to be your ideal helper.

- **To illustrate the relationship between Jesus and the church.** You represent Jesus in the church. Marriage is the role model of a relationship between Jesus and His church. The Bible states that Jesus is the bridegroom, and the church is the bride. Because of this, marriage is the divine illustration of the relationship between God and His people.

For example: a dysfunctional marriage or divorce is a poor illustration in the eyes of the world of the relationship between Jesus and the church.

The ingredients of a marriage pact are:

1. A legal relationship established by God

"¹⁴Yet you say, "For what reason?" Because the LORD has been witness between you and the wife of your youth, with whom you have dealt treacherously; yet she is your companion and your wife by covenant." Malachi 2.14

The word **"witness"** means to declare or affirm something as a witness. God is the one who witnesses your marriage vows. Some people believe that marriage is nothing more than a legal document, but when divorce seems inevitable, God is the accuser because marriage is a divine pact; not a human pact. Only God can break this pact.

"⁶So then, they are no longer two but one flesh. Therefore what God has joined together, let not man separate." Matthew 19.6

This verse is clear. God seals the union of two people in marriage.

One thing is to be legally married and quite another to be united by God. The ceremony, which takes place at the altar, is far more important than the legal ceremony.

The moment we say "yes" at the altar, God stamps His seal of approval on that "yes" from heaven. We can go to an earthly court and the judge signs the divorce request, but God says, "No!" from heaven. When you break the marriage covenant, be prepared for the consequences.

2. The marriage covenant is under authority

God is the supreme authority of your marriage, and the world needs to be bound to it. The order of authority is the following:

"*3But I want you to know that the head of every man is Christ, the head of woman is man, and the head of Christ is God.*" *1 Corinthians 11.3*

When you get married, it is not only what you and your spouse want to do, but also what God wants to do. Some believers get a divorce simply because their relationship has deteriorated. They can't get along, they don't understand each other or they don't feel the love they once felt. This action reflects the absence of the fear of God in their hearts. There are some men, and even ministers of the gospel, who council couples, advising them that divorce is the answer, but there is an established order of things such as: Jesus is the head of the man; therefore, man must submit himself to Jesus. Man is the head of the woman;

therefore, woman must submit to her husband. This order was not established to place one person in a superior position than the other, rather to establish divine order in marriage, thus providing a way for it to function properly.

3. The breaking of a divine pact is death

When a person breaks a divine pact, the consequence of this breakage is immediate death. There are curses that come upon the people who break a pact, but you might say, "Pastor, I am divorced and I'm still living, nothing has happened to me." No, you may not be dead, but I am sure that you are suffering the penalty of your divorce in other ways.

"16And the LORD God commanded the man, saying, "Of every tree of the garden you may freely eat; 17but of the tree of the knowledge of good and evil you shall not eat, for in the day that you eat of it you shall surely die." Genesis 2.16, 17

When Adam sinned he did not die a physical death, but his relationship with God was broken. In other words, his punishment was separation from God. There were also other consequences:

- "I will greatly multiply your sorrow and your conception; in pain you shall bring forth children."

- "Your desire shall be for your husband." The word desire means to control and manipulate. Women, regardless of how "holy" they might seem, will always have the desire to control her husband.

- "And he shall rule over you."

When you are emotionally "dead" in your marriage covenant, the life of God does not flow regardless of how much money you have. When you decide to divorce your spouse, the covenant with God is also broken and God's hand is removed from your life along with His blessings.

Is there a biblical reason for divorce?

Some people divorce their spouses today, and want my blessings for a new marriage ceremony to take place tomorrow. My answer is "no" because I don't want to kill them. A covenant can't be broken without consequences. The only Biblical reason for divorce is adultery and fornication. God forgives the sin of divorce if there is real repentance, but the consequences can't be avoided.

"19Honor your father and your mother, and, You shall love your neighbor as yourself." Matthew 19.9

Divorce has grave consequences; therefore, take time to seriously pray and ask God if this is a decision that you should take. When you keep the marriage covenant, you leave a wonderful inheritance for your children. If you are on the verge of a divorce, don't give up, keep fighting for your marriage, God will give you the victory.

God's covenant and blessings come together. If you remain in the covenant, the blessings will follow you. If you break the covenant or step outside of it, curses will follow. If you have a biblical reason for divorcing your spouse, then you can get out of your covenant and still receive His blessings, but if you don't have a biblical reason for divorce, then curses will overcome you for breaking the marriage covenant. Parents transfer their blessings to their children, and when the children obey and follow their parents, then they, too, will have something to transfer to the generations that follow after them.

God hates divorce.

"16For the LORD God of Israel says that He hates divorce, for it covers one's garment with violence," says the LORD of hosts. Therefore take heed to your spirit, that you do not deal treacherously." Malachi 2.16

The church needs to do something against divorce. The fear of God means to hate what God hates and to love what God loves. He hates divorce and loves the marriage covenant.

It is your responsibility as pastors to teach, guide and instruct your congregation on family values making sure that you cover the following areas: How to have a happy family, the roles and functions of each member, and how to teach and discipline the children.

CHAPTER 2

Marriage Breakers

$\mathcal{T}$his chapter will cover the different aspects of the family. You will learn about couples, singles, youth, the most common problems in the family, and more. Through the years in ministry, I have learned that the following plagues destroy the family:

1. Too many commitments and physical fatigue

You get involved in too many projects at school, the university, the workplace, at church, in sports, and in business. As you try to keep up with these commitments, your body becomes physically exhausted. Your personal agenda is so full that the time you spend with your family is extremely limited or non-existent.

What should you do to defeat this marriage breaker?

- You need to establish your priorities. Your family should be one of those priorities; you should always set time aside to spend quality time with your family. Some people have such heavy schedules that by the time they sit at the dinner table, they are too exhausted to enjoy their family or the meal.

"¹Unless the LORD builds the house, they labor in vain who build it; unless the LORD guards the city, the watchman stays awake in vain. ²It is vain for you to rise up early, to sit up late, to eat the bread of sorrows; for so He gives His beloved sleep." Psalms 127.1, 2

We live in a fast-paced, busy and agitated society. People rise out of bed before sunrise and lay down to sleep very late at night. They do not enjoy the fruit of their labor or their family. In our society, people end up losing their families and homes because of their none-stop commitments and overscheduled lives.

According to biblical standards, what should be the order of your priorities?

- **Your relationship with God.** Prior to going off to work, your business, or school, you should spend time with God in prayer to receive strength and guidance to do everything that is planned for the day. This should be your first priority.

- **Your relationship with the family.** After spending time with the Lord, you need to separate time from your busy schedules to spend quality time with your spouse and children. If these relationships are not nurtured, your marriages will suffer and weaken.

- **The church**. First, you spend quality time with God and with the family, and then you invest your time in the church. You should decide how to better assist, serve and contribute to the ministry with your spiritual gifts, talents and money.

- **The job.** Unfortunately, for most people, their careers are far more important than the others mentioned. Because their careers are a priority, their lives are up-side down. Their homes are in disarray and many are contemplating divorce.

2. Spending money unwisely

Disorder in the finance department is one of the greatest causes for divorce. Did you know that eighty percent of the people in prison are doing time for crimes that have to do with money? Three out of ten marriages break up because of financial problems. Also, the conclusion has been reached that, for the most part, people who are experiencing financial difficulties don't know how to handle their finances properly or have terrible administration practices. Many people within the church do not plan for their futures. These concepts teaches that those expenditures and disorganized financial planning is an effective marriage breaker, but don't dismay, you are about to learn the biblical solution to your financial situation and how to organize them.

Who should be in charge of the checkbook, the man or the woman?

- **The man.** The husband is the breadwinner in the family; therefore, he should have the responsibility of handling the family's finances. Of course, there are exceptions to every rule. If the man of the house doesn't have the ability or talent to handle the finances properly, if he is wasteful in his spending, or irresponsible in making timely payments to creditors, then he should delegate this responsibility to his wife. This decision should be taken only after the husband and wife mutually agrees to this arrangement.

How should the family's budget be prepared and distributed?

One reason why many people fail financially is because they never prepared a budget that was in line with their earnings. Without this budget, people distribute their finances unwisely, usually, according to their personal priorities and not the family's.

The family's basic expenses are divided into three categories:

❑ **Basic needs.** When the income check is received, the family's basic living expenses must be paid for at once.

What are these basic needs?

- ◆ Tithes and offerings
- ◆ Food
- ◆ Clothing
- ◆ Rent
- ◆ Water
- ◆ Light

These basic needs should be a priority. They need to be paid before other expenses.

❑ **Luxuries.** These are things that you would love to have for personal enjoyment; these are not needed to survive, but they make living a lot more enjoyable. For instance:

- ◆ Telephone
- ◆ Television, cable
- ◆ Car
- ◆ Brand name clothing

❑ **Wishes.** These are things that you don't need, but that you desire to have just because you like them or want them for your personal pleasure.

- ◆ Vacations and trips
- ◆ Boat
- ◆ Sports cars
- ◆ Designer clothes
- ◆ Sports

A word of advice: spend your money wisely.

- **Avoid worldly things.** You should be striving for God's promotions and approval, not things that lack integrity like illegal programs or activities that eventually destroy your personal testimony, your money and your credibility. Always keep in mind the law of sowing and reaping, that which you sow, you shall also reap.

"⁴Do not overwork to be rich; because of your own understanding, cease! ⁵Will you set your eyes on that which is not? For riches certainly make themselves wings; they fly away like an eagle toward heaven." Proverbs 23.4, 5

- **Keep your finances up to date.** Never do anything that can endanger your financial future, including purchases and investments that have not been thoroughly investigated and researched.

Never depend on future events for your financial stability, and learn to sacrifice your personal desires and wants if necessary.

"28For which of you, intending to build a tower, does not sit down first and count the cost, whether he has enough to finish it." Luke 14.28

Before investing your money, you should ask yourself the following questions:

- ✓ Will this purchase help prosper God's Kingdom through me?
- ✓ Is this purchase really necessary?
- ✓ Can I live without this?
- ✓ Is this the best possible buy?
- ✓ Will this purchase improve the quality of the relationships in my family?
- ✓ Will it depreciate quickly?
- ✓ Is what I am buying going to require expensive maintenance?

- **Instead of loaning your money, give it away.** When you give something as a gift, it becomes a greater testimony for the person receiving the gift. Share God's blessings with others.

- **Avoid being a lender.** The Bible is clear on this subject; you should never be a lender to others.

"¹My son, if you become surety for your friend, if you have shaken hands in pledge for a stranger, ²you are snared by the words of your mouth; you are taken by the words of your mouth. ³So do this, my son, and deliver yourself; for you have come into the hand of your friend: go and humble yourself; plead with your friend. ⁴Give no sleep to your eyes, nor slumber to your eyelids. ⁵Deliver yourself like a gazelle from the hand of the hunter, and like a bird from the hand of the fowler."
Proverbs 6.1-5

"¹⁸A man devoid of understanding shakes hands in a pledge, and becomes surety for his friend."
Proverbs 17.18

Every time you become a lender to someone else, you are disobeying the Word of God.

• **Your decision to buy something should be based on the following:** do you need it; is it an unnecessary luxury or is it something you want. Make sure you take the time to think about what you are buying before spending your money. The time you take to think about your purchase will help you to make the right decision and will always guarantee that you will spend your money wisely.

• **Never make financial decisions under pressure or in haste.** Usually, the sales representatives in the places you shop will try to motivate or pressure you into making a quick decision to buy their products. They pressure you with lies and offers that seem as if you can't pass them up because the offers will never be offered again. Please, never make a decision under this type of peer pressure.

- **If you feel uneasy and restless about the purchase, don't buy it.** Many people make decisions too quickly, in haste, and as a result, they fail to accomplish what they started to do, which was to invest their money wisely. Peace is a great way for God to talk to you and let you know if what you are buying is a good decision or a bad one. If you are not at peace with the purchase you are about to make, then this is God's way of telling you that it is a bad investment.

The Biblical way for a couple to prosper is through their tithes and offerings. If you choose not to practice this principle, then get ready to face financial disaster.

3. Selfishness

A selfish person is easily identified. He usually looks out for number one. Selfishness is completely opposite to love.

It is impossible to avoid confrontation and friction in a marriage when one spouse is giving one hundred percent of the time, and the other spouse sits back and receives without giving. When the husband and wife both love to receive and not give, this selfish attitude quickly ends up in marital disaster.

Where does selfishness come from? The selfish attitude is present, when the old man is still present in you. It is identified by the fact that your only desire or intention is to seek self-gratification. This could be a sign that you are not born again. This is a major marriage breaker. Selfishness, self-gratification and personal want and needs destroy the marriage and deceive people into believing that divorce is the answer to their problems or a way out of their unhappy marriage without regard to their children. You need to learn how to die to your selfish desires and begin to place the welfare of your loved ones before your own. You should give sacrificially, expecting nothing in return, sharing your love with those around you and learning to love the way God loves you, with agape love.

There are two types of people in this world.

- **Those who give.** This type of person places more importance on the needs of others before his own. He gives unconditionally and loves doing it.

- **Those who receive.** Most couples that end up in divorce were involved in a marriage relationship where one partner was the receiver of the other partner's attention, love and care; the receiver rarely or never reciprocated that love and attention.

What is the answer to selfishness?

- **Place the needs of others above yourself.**

"23Then He said to them all, "If anyone desires to come after Me, let him deny himself, and take up his cross daily, and follow Me." Luke 9.23

Blessed is the one who gives unconditionally, then he who receives. Make a daily commitment to deny the selfish desires of your flesh by placing the needs of others above yourself; look for ways to bless the people around you.

- **Walk in love.**

"4Love suffers long and is kind; love does not envy; love does not parade itself, is not puffed up; 5does not behave rudely, does not seek its own, is not provoked, thinks no evil; 6does not rejoice in iniquity, but rejoices in the truth; 7bears all things, believes all things, hopes all things, endures all things." 1 Corinthians 13.4-7

Begin to look for ways to bless the people around you and put aside all selfish desires.

4. Lack of communication

Lack of communication is a major marriage breaker. How can you deal with this problem? What causes the breakup of communication in the home?

- **Lack of respect.** Respect is lost when one spouse refuses to honor the other by not honoring his or her role in the home.

- **Shouting and screaming.** It is extremely difficult for a husband to tolerate his wife when she shouts and screams while trying to get her point across. Neither of them should raise their voices because this attitude or reaction to a difficult situation opens the door for the enemy to crawl right into the relationship and destroy the marriage by making the problem seem bigger than it really is.

- **Verbal abuse.** For instance, when the husband mistreats or abuses his wife verbally with hurtful and offensive words, the wife will immediately close her self off by shutting down the communication process.

- **To assume the spouse's role or responsibility.** When one spouse takes over the other's role or responsibility in the home, it prevents the communication process from flowing in the relationship.

- **Being a terrible listener.** Each time a spouse wants to speak, but is constantly interrupted by the other's comments, which contradicts what is being said before he or she has a chance to express his or her thoughts or needs, this creates major conflicts in the marriage relationship. A terrible listener is also a person who doesn't give the other the time of day, who turns his or her back to the needs of the spouse and one who believes that what the other person has to say is not important. This attitude makes a bad situation worse and causes hurt feelings in one or both spouses because one person didn't take the time to listen.

"¹⁹ So then, my beloved brethren, let every man be swift to hear, slow to speak, slow to wrath." James 1.19

What is the solution to a lack of communication in the home?

- **Learn to be a good listener.** When you learn to listen, you are able to offer the other person good advice and feedback. It gives you time to think about what you are going to say. It is also a great way to avoid major conflict in the relationship because you take time to pay attention to the other person's needs.

- **Learn to speak only what needs to be said and then be straight forward about it.** Never assume that the other person knows what you are in need of, what you're thinking or feeling; they can't read your mind. You must learn to speak what is in your heart, clearly and straightforward.

- **Learn to express what you feel at the proper time.**

"23A man has joy by the answer of his mouth, and a word spoken in due season, how good it is!"
Proverbs 15.23

Most emotions or feelings should be expressed immediately. Putting off expressing your feelings will change your perspective of the truth later on.

- **Make sure that you say exactly how you feel.** When you talk to someone, is it your intention to convey your emotions, feelings, needs, thoughts or observations? If you are unsure of what you want to say, then what comes out of your mouth will be confused and distorted. You must make sure that the words that come out of your mouth represent the exact thing that you want to communicate.

In chapter five of this book, the subject on communication will be further studied.

5. Sexual frustration

When one spouse is not sexually satisfied, the doors to the enemy are widely opened for the devil to induce the desire of infidelity in the dissatisfied spouse; as you well know, this is never the answer or the right path to take.

What causes sexual frustration?

- **Physical and sexual abuse.** If a husband, who physically or sexually abuses his wife, wants to engage in sexual intimacy he will find that his wife is unable to respond to his needs because the only thing on her mind is the pain and memory of the abuse. Women are severely and emotionally affected by physical and sexual abuse because they were created to react to tenderness, love and words of affirmation, not physical or verbal abuse, especially from their husbands.

- **Rape or incest.** When the husband or wife has experienced the trauma of a rape, incest or sexual molestation, and these emotional wounds have not been properly dealt with and healed, the spirit of frigidness and even fear overcome the individual. The painful memory of the trauma makes it impossible for the hurting individual to react lovingly and willingly to sexual intimacy.

- **The absence of the "Eros" kind of love.** For a couple to experience sexual satisfaction, the "Eros" kind of love must be present in the relationship. "Eros" is erotic love given by God to the married couple, which makes the sexual relationship successful and enjoyable. In some instances, this kind of love is lost in the marriage relationship. If this is happening in your marriage, ask God to renew your desire for each other. He will do it.

- **Pornography, gambling and other addictions.** When one spouse is addicted to pornography, he or she will want their spouse to respond or satisfy their needs according to this type of stimuli. If the spouse is unwilling to respond to this approach to sexual intimacy, then the person with the addiction will feel sexually frustrated and begin to look for someone else who can satisfy his or her depraved needs. Other addictions such as drugs and gambling also affect the marriage relationship and cause thousands of people to choose divorce as a way out.

- **When one spouse refuses to be sexually intimate.** The Word of God says that it is a sin to deprive your spouse of sexual intimacy. Many couples are very frustrated because one spouse refuses or rarely accepts the sexual invitation of the other.

"⁵Do not deprive one another except with consent for a time, that you may give yourselves to fasting and prayer; and come together again so that Satan does not tempt you because of your lack of self-control."
1 Corinthians 7.5

What are the solutions to sexual frustration?

- **Christian counseling.** Only the Word of God can help you find the answers to your problems. Godly words of encouragement will help you to make the necessary changes for a successful marital relationship. Look for a Christian counselor who can give you godly advice for your difficult situations.

- **Inner healing and deliverance.** Sometimes the root of the problem to your sexual frustration could be spiritual. Until this is properly dealt with, your situation will remain unchanged. You need to make an appointment to receive inner healing and deliverance.

6. Failed business ventures

Bad business decisions, the closing of a business, and hard times at work will cause frustration, anger and irritability. Often these emotions are directly expressed to the family in a negative way causing terrible problems and even the destruction of the home and marriage.

7. Success in business

Although success in business seems like an unlikely marriage breaker, it is almost as risky as a failed business venture. Being a successful businessperson is worthless if you lose your family in the process. This is the very reason why your priorities must be in their proper order. While it is great to want success in business, your priority should always be the success of your family. If success is the result of sacrificing your time with God and your family, then what you have will not satisfy you. You won't be able to enjoy it.

"[13]There is a severe evil which I have seen under the sun: riches kept for their owner to his hurt. [14]But those riches perish through misfortune; when he begets a son, there is nothing in his hand." Ecclesiastes 5.13, 14

"[19]As for every man to whom God has given riches and wealth, and given him power to eat of it, to receive his heritage and rejoice in his labor--this is the gift of God." Ecclesiastes 5.19

While it is important to enjoy everything that you have attained, it is more important to love and safeguard your family.

8. Married at a young age

Statistics show that young people that enter into marriage between the ages of seventeen and twenty have the highest risk of divorce then those who get married between the ages of twenty-one and twenty-five. We are living in a society that influence people to believe that marriage is nothing more than living together and if it doesn't work out, then divorce is acceptable.

When are young people ready to get married?

- **When Jesus is the center of their lives.** In other words, when they are in love with Jesus, when He is Lord of their lives, when they serve Him and live according to His Word; then they are ready to get married.

- **When they are financially stable.** Many young people are not financially stable to pay for their own expenses. Either they don't have a job, or if they do, they don't earn enough. If they don't have enough to financially support themselves, then they are not ready for marriage.

- **When their careers are established.** I strongly believe that young people have the capacity to be spiritual and intellectual. When a person graduates with a diploma in the field or career of his choice, his chance at finding good job and of getting better wages are much greater than those who never went to school or quit half-way into their education.

- **When they are emotionally stable.** If young people are dependant on the guidance and opinions of their parents before making a decision, then this is indicative of emotional immaturity. Young people need to be emotionally mature and stable before making the decision to assume the responsibilities of a serious relationship such as marriage.

I strongly believe that the information in this book will help every young person who is considering marriage. These will help them prevent the major mistakes that others have made before them.

Young people often get married for the wrong reasons:

- **Pregnancy.** A pastoral advice to all parents: never force your daughter to get married if she is not in love with the father of her child. A forced marriage because of pregnancy is always a mistake. Remember that two wrongs don't make a right.

- **To get away from their parents.** Dysfunctional families will make the children want to leave home as quickly as possible. Many young people believe that running away from their problems at home is the answer, and according to their confused way of thinking, the answer to their family situation is marriage, but you and I both know that this is a terrible mistake.

- **Loneliness.** Some young people feel alone and unloved, which causes them to make the mistake of getting married to end their loneliness. They ignore the fact that marriage is not the answer to their loneliness and make a wrong decision.

- **Hormones.** Young people will be motivated to react to their hormonal changes if they are not completely committed and dedicated to God. Their hormones will push them into making wrong decisions and to act irrationally.

9. The in-laws

It is established in the Word of God that when a person decides to get married, that he and she should leave their mother and father. When this Biblical principle is ignored or violated, divorce is almost inevitable.

"24Therefore a man shall leave his father and mother and be joined to his wife, and they shall become one flesh." Genesis 2.24

Many children are still dependent on their parents, but they need to remember that once they make the decision to get married, their commitment is to their spouse, not mom or dad. Unfortunately, the emotional and spiritual dependence of the kids prevents them from learning to live independently, which eventually affects their marriage.

Living with your in-laws is to risk ending up in divorce.

What is the answer to this problem?

If at all possible, don't live with your in-laws and take control of your family. When families live independent of their in-laws, the husband feels respected and the wife feels secure because there are no outside influences or unwanted advice. If, and when, you are in need of godly advice, make an appointment to speak with your pastor, a leader in your church or any other responsible person.

Unfounded jealousy

Many divorces are caused by unfounded jealousy. People who are jealous are being influenced by the enemy to see things that are not real.

There are two types of jealousy:

- **Demonic jealousy.** This type of jealousy is based on insecurity and fear. It is perverse and it causes divorce. The person who feels this type of unfounded jealousy is already experiencing the punishment of insecurity and fear of someone coming along and taking away the person they love.

"³⁴For jealousy is a husband's fury; therefore he will not spare in the day of vengeance." Proverbs 6.34

- **Holy zeal.**

"⁵...you shall not bow down to them nor serve them. For I, the LORD your God, am a jealous God, visiting the iniquity of the fathers upon the children to the third and fourth generations of those who hate Me." Exodus 20.5

God is a jealous God. This type of jealousy or zeal protects what belongs to you; it is not based on insecurity or fear, but rather it is based on love. In other words, "He is jealous because He loves you." Is it proper to feel jealousy when it comes to your spouse?" Yes, but only if this jealousy or zeal is the kind that rises up when danger is ahead and not unfounded jealousy based on a misguided imagination.

"⁵Or do you think that the Scripture says in vain, "The Spirit who dwells in us yearns jealously?" James 4.5

The Lord is jealous when His children love the world more than they love Him.

People with an out-of-control kind of jealousy hold on to what they have using manipulative and controlling methods in an effort to prevent losing it.

What are the character traits of a jealous person?

- Possessive
- Manipulative and controlling
- Selfish
- Insecure
- Fearful

Why are some people jealous?

There are several reasons why a person might feel jealousy, including traumas, past emotional wounds, rejection of his or her parents, abandonment or great differences in age (when one spouse feels too old or too young to be with the spouse).

What is the solution to jealousy?

- **Learning to trust in God.** Trusting in God means to completely yield or surrender to God without reservations. Surrender your family and yourself to God, trust Him.

- **Renounce the spirit of jealousy.** The spirit of jealousy begins to affect people when there are traumas and emotional wounds from the past that have not been dealt with properly. Deliverance is necessary before they can be free from this spirit; it restores the trust that was lost in the marriage relationship.

There are many more marriage breakers to discuss, but I have chosen to share with you the most common. Unfortunately, many of these marriage breakers are also affecting Christian families and relationships. It is imperative to do a self-analysis to see if any of these elements are present in your relationships with your family and spouse. If you can identify any of these in you, then you need to get rid of them completely and begin to develop strong relationships again. You must correct what you are doing wrong, and the only way to accomplish this is to repent and to seek God's divine intervention in your life.

CHAPTER 3

The Differences Between Men and Women

will begin this chapter on the emotional and spiritual structure of a woman.

The composition of a woman

- **Intuition**. The woman is like the spiritual radar, able to discern all things. A woman can discern when something is about to happen; she has greater discernment than a man does.

- **Sensible.** Women are far more sensible then men to the needs and wants of others.

  Sensibility and intuition are given by God to help her feel more secure and loved.

- **Women enjoy sexual relationships differently.** Women enjoy sexual intimacy for different reasons than men. She is motivated to be intimate because of an internal need; she needs romance, intimacy, tenderness and gentleness. For a woman to enjoy sexual intimacy, and before she can achieve her orgasm, it is important for her to hear loving words from her husband and to feel his tender and gentle touch. It is impossible for her to be sexually aroused until she receives verbal and physical love, and affirmation.

The composition of a man

- **Man is logical.** Man, on the other hand, is more practical when making decisions. He takes into consideration reason and logic while the woman looks at the spiritual side of things. Women have the tendency to focus on the smallest details and men go directly to the heart of the matter.

- **Man is less sensitive.** Man must learn to develop his sensitive side. Women are sensitive to the needs of others while men remain unaware of them.

- **He enjoys sexuality for different reasons.** Men want sexual intimacy because of an external or physical need. He is attracted by what he sees; it helps him to want and enjoy sex more.

- **He communicates less than a woman does.** After many counseling sessions with couples, I find that men have less to say, thus frustrating their wives who want to share everything.

Physical differences between men and women:

Man	Woman
• Greater bone density	• Smaller bone structure
• More blood (4.7 liters)	• Less blood (3.5 liters)
• Wider shoulders	• Narrow shoulders
• Greater physical strength (40% more)	• Less physical strength
• Man only uses one hemisphere of his brain, which makes him a logical being.	• Women use both hemispheres of the brain, which makes her more intuitive.
• Man's skin is less sensitive and delicate.	• A woman's skin is seven times more sensible and delicate.
• Narrow hips	• Wide hips
• Men speak an average of 2,500 words per hour.	• Women speak an average of 5,000 words per hour.

Why are they different?

Men and women were created different to complement each other. Few couples take advantage of their differences to improve their lives. In the midst of such diversity among the sexes, it is possible to have unity; these differences complement each other.

There are four different types of temperament: melancholic, choleric, phlegmatic and sanguine. Although everyone has a combination of temperaments, there is usually one that rises above the rest. In other words, even though an individual has traces of having a phlegmatic temperament, he will be considered choleric because the traits of this temperament overshadow those of the phlegmatic. Some of these temperaments complement each other, such as sanguine and phlegmatic. The sanguine is impulsive, hyperactive, extroverted and talkative, but the phlegmatic is level-headed, calmer, self-controlled and usually takes his time to accomplish his tasks. If a person with a sanguine temperament marries a person with a phlegmatic temperament, they will compliment each other. It is imperative to know and understand which temperament we are so that we can complement each other better.

Differences become the unifying factor

Marital unity is made up of three areas:

"24Therefore a man shall leave his father and mother and be joined to his wife, and they shall become one flesh." Genesis 2.24

- Spiritual
- Emotional
- Physical

Spiritual unity. *"Shall become one flesh."* Which elements are important to keep in mind when we desire spiritual unity?

- **A Christ-centered home.**

"²¹For all seek their own, not the things which are of Christ Jesus." Philippians 2.21

In a Christ-centered home both partners follow Christ and not their own needs and wants. The reason why you need to have spiritual unity is to enable you to establish a home where the goal is to exalt the name of Jesus and not the individual. You need to pray together, not only as a couple, but also together with your children, to serve together and do God's will. A home where Christ is not Lord will fail. Jesus should be the number one priority in your homes; if Jesus is not first, nothing will work out right.

- **Build an altar for the Lord.**

"³⁰Then Elijah said to all the people, "Come near to me." So all the people came near to him. And he repaired the altar of the LORD that was broken down." 1 Kings 18.30

Altar: This is the place of praise and worship where the entire family gathers together to worship God.

Your behavior is the end result of your relationship with God. As you continue to pray and seek God, the easier it will become to control the desires of your flesh, which include anger, rage, arrogance and pride. If the altar has fallen, rebuild it again!

There is a great problem in our great nation and that is the shortage of time. You must make every effort to spend time with God and to build an altar to the Lord together with your family. Prayer holds the family together. You need to have your individual altar with God, and also an altar where the family gathers together to worship Him, pray and read His Word.

- **Spiritual unity for the vision and the calling of God for your spouse.**

  Perhaps you are not very enthusiastic of your spouse's calling, but God gave you your spouse as a partner. You need to be supportive of his or her calling and back them up when they need you. One day, you will be held accountable for your spouse before God. You are responsible for your spouse's calling (the calling is your spouse's vocation).

If you are unable to achieve spiritual unity as a couple, then it will be almost impossible to be in agreement in the emotional and physical areas of your relationship. When the marriage is based solely on physical attraction and emotional needs, then the marriage is founded on sand instead of on the rock.

When spiritual unity is present in the marriage relationship, the problems that rise up in the emotional or physical area will be dealt with effectively.

The power in spiritual unity

"[19]Again I say to you that if two of you agree on earth concerning anything that they ask, it will be done for them by My Father in heaven." Matthew 18.19

The enemy hates when couples stand together in agreement and unity because when they do, they are powerful in everything they set their minds on. To achieve spiritual unity, you need to be in agreement in your spiritual beliefs, you need to seek peace, work together, deny the desires of your flesh and you must walk in love.

God created men and women differently to compliment each other. You must make every effort to agree in everything. This will benefit your family, your marriage, your children and it will glorify God.

Emotional unity

To have emotional unity is to understand each other's feelings, wishes, dreams, likes and dislikes, goals, and more. Every couple should know his or her spouse's strengths and weaknesses in order to effectively join forces and become strong supporters of each other. This opens the door to better understanding and communication in the relationship.

Physical unity

Physical unity is the consummation of the spiritual and the emotional areas of the relationship; it seals the expression of love. God created men and women differently to compliment each other and become one flesh, in body, soul and spirit.

CHAPTER 4

Responsibilities, Roles and Functions of Men and Women

$\mathcal{W}$ hen we speak of roles and responsibilities, we are talking about the individual functions of each spouse in the home. Few spouses understand what their function, role or responsibility is in their relationship; this causes great problems in the marriage. Before we go into defining what the man's or woman's role in the home is, it is important to know what their needs are.

What a woman wants:

- **Love** – Throughout Scripture, God tells man that he should love his wife.

- *"25Husbands, love your wives, just as Christ also loved the church and gave Himself for her, 26that He might sanctify and cleanse her with the washing of water by the word, 27that He might present her to Himself a glorious church, not having spot or wrinkle or any such thing, but that she should be holy and without blemish. 28So husbands ought to love their own wives as their own bodies; he who loves his wife loves himself." Ephesians 5.25-28*

- **Security** – Women want to feel secure. There are three areas where a woman really needs to feel secure: in her spiritual values, the moral standards in the home and in the finances.

- **Protection** – When a woman gets married, she sees her husband as her protector, the same way she considered her father to be her defender. By nature, the woman needs this protective covering; it is one of her basic needs.

What a man wants:

- **Respect** – This is extremely important for a man. This statement becomes evident in the fact that many men are willing to lie, kill, steal or do whatever it takes to have people's respect.

"[33]Nevertheless let each one of you in particular so love his own wife as himself, and let the wife see that she respects her husband." Ephesians 5.33

Man's greatest fear is to lose people's respect, especially his wife's and children's.

What is respect? It means to honor, to give someone his proper place. Every woman should support her husband; work together with him without taking his place.

The following is a list of ways the wife shows disrespect to her husband:

- When she raises her voice
- When she makes spiritual and financial decisions that affect the home and relationship without consulting her husband
- When she disagrees with her husband and tells him to be quiet in public
- When she criticizes her husband in public
- When she doesn't support his authority with the children

When you love someone, you want to be able to rely on his or her respect, but as you really get to know them, it gets harder to maintain the same level of respect because by this time you are already familiar with their weaknesses.

- **Admiration.** A man wants to be admired in the things that he does as the leader of the home. When the woman feels loved and secure, and the man feels respected and admired, then, each one will begin to function properly in their marital roles.

What are the man's role and responsibilities as a husband?

From the beginning of creation, we see that God created man and gave him a place of honor, to be lord over everything, and He created woman to be his ideal helper. The man must take the initiative to begin to fulfill his roles or functions; as a result, the woman will be compelled to follow.

Responsibilities of a man

1. The man must love his wife

Scripture tells us that men should love their wives. Being loved is one of a woman's basic necessities.

"25Husbands, love your wives, just as Christ also loved the church and gave Himself for her." Ephesians 5.25

How should a man love a woman?

- **With spoken expressions of love.** Always and at all times, man should be expressing words of affirmation towards his wife, such as: "You look beautiful today," "Dinner was delicious," "I love you," "You are very special," and more.

- **Emotional love.** The woman experiences difficult times in her life when she will need her husband's emotional love or support. It is important for the husband to offer his emotional support during menopause, pregnancy, delivery and any other time she might need it.

• **Physical love.** The husband should demonstrate his love for his wife with physical touch such as hugs, caressing, kisses, etc. This small demonstration of love makes the woman feel secure. When the husband shows his love, the wife answers with submission.

2. Spiritual Priest or spiritual leader in the home

"³But I want you to know that the head of every man is Christ, the head of woman is man, and the head of Christ is God. ⁴Every man praying or prophesying, having his head covered, dishonors his head." 1 Corinthians 11.3, 4

Priest or leader. A priest is responsible for the spiritual, individual and congregational development of his family. The spiritual leader sets the spiritual boundaries in the home. A good leader makes sure that all things work together for the well-being of the family; he is the head of the household; the one that takes the responsibility and makes decisions. The husband should be far more consecrated than his wife.

What are the man's responsibilities as the priest or spiritual leader?

- **The man should be the first to give his tithes.** The blessings and organization of a home depend on the head of the household. When the man sets the example in giving the tithes and offering, then God blesses the home financially.

- **The man should be the first to pray.**

  "⁸I desire therefore that the men pray everywhere, lifting up holy hands, without wrath and doubting."
  1 Timothy 2.8

  Men should take the initiative to pray and seek God; the family will follow after him.

- **The man should be the first to worship.** When the man constantly worships God, whether at home or at church, the woman feels secure. She responds to this with respect and admiration.

The body of Christ is in great shortage of spirit-filled men. Women are usually the ones to serve and be intercessors at church, and the ones to carry the burden of the spiritual development in the home.

Most marital problems exist because the husband is not fulfilling his function as the spiritual leader in the home.

3. The emotional provider in the home

"⁷But we were gentle among you, just as a nursing mother cherishes her own children."
1 Thessalonians 2.7

The one who provides the emotional stability is the one who helps build the character of an individual. One role or function of the husband in the home is to build his family's character with words of affirmation and encouragement. Sometimes, a member of the family might be suffering from low self-esteem, it is then that the husband and father, the one who provides emotional stability, comes in to show his support and to emotionally restore and affirm his family.

When should a man protect and provide for his family the most? He should provide unconditional emotional support during moments of crisis, sickness, sadness, etc. He should demonstrate and give his unconditional love and support.

The word **"sustain"** means to nourish until maturity is achieved. Your emotional support doesn't end until the moment a person reaches maturity. When a husband provides emotional support, his wife will respond with respect and admiration.

The woman **needs** more emotional support than the man does during three stages of her life:

- During her menstrual cycle
- During and after pregnancy
- During menopause

Children need to be affirmed and encouraged during their development years. You need to stop cursing your children with your negative words. If you are the provider of emotional stability, then you must strengthen their self-esteem.

4. The financial provider in the home

The financial provider supplies the financial needs of the family. To be a good provider, you must be an excellent worker. God doesn't bless lazy people.

"¹⁰Whatever your hand finds to do, do it with your might; for there is no work or device or knowledge or wisdom in the grave where you are going." Ecclesiastes 9.10

There are many "Christian" men today who don't provide for their families. These are worse then unbelievers.

"⁸But if anyone does not provide for his own, and especially for those of his household, he has denied the faith and is worse than an unbeliever." 1 Timothy 5.8

If you want God's blessings to become a better provider, then you must do the following:

- You must have the desire to work.

  "²⁴The fear of the wicked will come upon him, and the desire of the righteous will be granted." Proverbs 10.24

- You must be strong.

  "⁶Be strong and of good courage, for to this people you shall divide as an inheritance the land which I swore to their fathers to give them." Joshua 1.6

When the husband is not a provider, it makes his wife and children feel insecure and unprotected.

5. The protector of the family

The protector safeguards his family physically and spiritually. A husband and father who is a protector or guardian cares for his family during moments of crisis and fights to provide a better education for his children.

The husband and father who protects his family provides security and assurance. If a man is himself insecure or double-minded when it comes to making decisions, then he will be unable to provide the emotional stability and protection that his family needs. Men that are selfish, indecisive and immature can't provide security for their family.

6. The progenitor of the home

Man is responsible for the four generations that come after him. These four generations depend on the wise or bad decisions that man makes. Men are responsible for their children. You need to make wise decisions today so that you don't have to be sorry tomorrow.

7. Developer and cultivator

Every man was created by God to develop and cultivate everything that comes from him. God gave him a commandment, to cultivate the land. We strongly believe that if man does his job well, he will end up with a different woman than the one that he married. Why? Because when he married her she was a certain way, but later on, as time passed, and as man cultivated or sowed into her positive changes, she begins to change and improve in every area of her life. Then, it is correct to say that he came to the end of his life with the same woman, but with a different attitude and outlook on life.

When the man makes the decision to take the initiative to fulfill his role, function and responsibilities in the home, then the woman will choose to follow him with joy.

Responsibilities of a woman

1. The woman must be the ideal helper to her husband

"18 And the LORD God said, "It is not good that man should be alone; I will make him a helper comparable to him." Genesis 2.18

Before we define what her responsibilities are, we must understand what the word "helper" means:

Helper – It is the Hebrew word *"ezer,"* meaning to enclose, surround, protect and help during times of crisis and difficulty. Therefore, God created the woman to protect, help, enclose and surround her husband during times of crisis. A helper also means someone who is the same.

Many women are doing exactly the opposite. Instead of being the ideal helper, they criticize and hurt their husbands. There are times when the man needs a woman's prayer and support, especially during difficult financial situations or when he makes the wrong decision. Instead of criticizing him, protect him and support him in prayer.

Woman was created and called to be the ideal helper, to work side by side with her husband, but not to do the man's job. The wise woman knows how to encourage her husband during moments of failure.

2. The woman must submit herself to her husband

"²²Wives, submit to your own husbands, as to the Lord. ²³For the husband is head of the wife, as also Christ is head of the church; and He is the Savior of the body. ²⁴Therefore, just as the church is subject to Christ, so let the wives be to their own husbands in everything." Ephesians 5.22-24

The meaning of the word "submission" has been twisted and misinterpreted, that is why when the woman hears this word she feels terrified.

Contrary to what most people understand submission to mean, the word submission is actually a really good word with an awesome blessing; Christ was submissive to His Father's will.

Following is a list of erroneous concepts concerning submission:

- Submission has nothing to do with inequality or inferiority. Jesus is the same as God and His submission did not make Him inferior to His Father. The woman doesn't become inferior to man when she submits to him.

"26For you are all sons of God through faith in Christ Jesus. 27For as many of you as were baptized into Christ have put on Christ. 28There is neither Jew nor Greek, there is neither slave nor free, there is neither male nor female; for you are all one in Christ Jesus."
Galatians 3.26-28

Men and women are the same in God's eyes, therefore, when a woman submits to her husband it does not make her less than who she is.

- Women, submission to your husbands does not mean that you are his property. He does not have the right to use you like a rug (under his feet). You are not inferior to him. You are God's children and you need to be submissive to your husbands, as unto God, to fulfill God's purpose in your family. Jesus was submissive to His Father to fulfill the plan of Salvation.

- Submission doesn't imply that you have to agree with everything that your husband says or does. It does mean that you should recognize his position in the home as the head of the household and that he was given this responsibility to fulfill God's plan for the family.

In essence, we are the same, but in function, we are different.

Perhaps you don't always agree with your employer, but you submit to him. Or you might not agree with the judge's sentence, but you submit and accept his decision. More than submission to an individual, you submit yourself to a "position". God called your husband and placed him in the position as head of your home and family.

What is the meaning of Biblical submission?

Submission is to be teachable and adaptable to an authority figure. It means to respond to someone else's love. When a woman feels her husband's love, she responds by submitting to him and adapting to his authority.

The difference between obedience and submission is:

Obedience means to obey authority out of fear and to avoid paying the consequences.

Submission means to submit to authority with a joyful and pleasant attitude; this attitude helps you to be teachable and adaptable.

Remember that the key for a woman to submit to her husband is found in the man himself. When the wife feels loved by her husband, it is easier for her to submit and to obey. Obedience is relative, but submission is absolute.

How far should a woman go in her submission to her husband?

"22 Wives, submit to your own husbands, as to the Lord. 23For the husband is head of the wife, as also Christ is head of the church; and He is the Savior of the body. 24Therefore, just as the church is subject to Christ, so let the wives be to their own husbands in everything." Ephesians 5.22-24

"In everything," "...as to the Lord." Women, this is the key to your submission. When a man stops walking in Christ, he is no longer holding the role of head of the home. Never disobey God to follow your husband, but if your husband is working to serve God, then don't oppose him. If he is trying to apply Sunday's sermon, then help him to accomplish it. Perhaps he is doing a lousy job, maybe he is not very good at it, but at least he is trying, you need to give him credit for that and help him because he needs it.

Every woman should say to her husband, "Starting today, you are my leader. God placed you above me as the head of our home. I will honor you and submit to you. I will follow you as the leader and head of our family. I only ask one thing from you, my love, that you never try to separate me from God. If you do, if you try to separate me from God, I will be forced to leave you and follow my first love, God. I don't want to leave you, but if you follow after my first love, then I will follow Him and you."

Every husband needs to hear these words spoken by his wife. He needs to realize that every where else he is just an ordinary person, but at home he is the king of his castle.

Which two areas should the woman never submit to?

- If your husband asks you to do something that makes you feel uncomfortable, then you should not submit.

- When your husband stops being the head of the home. In other words, when he no longer serves the Lord and begins to compromise God's Word. For instance, if your husband wants you to stop going to church because he doesn't want to go, then you can't obey this request; otherwise you will be going against the will of God. If you obey his request, then your family and home will be destroyed.

Why is it so difficult for a woman to submit?

- **Abusive authority figure from the past.** When a woman is a witness to the abuse of her father against her mother or any other type of abuse by someone in authority in her life, then she finds it very difficult to submit to her husband. What is the solution to the problem? Inner healing and deliverance.

- **The curse of the original sin**.

"16To the woman He said, I will greatly multiply your grief and your suffering in pregnancy and the pangs of childbearing; with spasms of distress you will bring forth children. Yet your desire and craving will be for your husband, and he will rule over you." Genesis 3.16

Adam and Eve's disobedience in the Garden of Eden had terrible consequences. As you already know, Eve was told that her desire would be for her husband, to control him, and Adam's desire was to be lord over everything. To help us understand this concept, first we need to define the meaning of the word "desire":

The word **"desire"** means to manipulate, control and dominate. This is a woman's nature, to control, manipulate and dominate her husband. However, man's desire is to have lordship over his wife, to subdue her and be a type of dictator over her. The woman, on the other hand, regardless of how "holy" and righteous she might be, she will always have the desire to control her husband. This is the consequence of the original sin. When the woman understands that it is in her nature to reject the thought of submission to her husband, she will need to ask the Holy Spirit for His help.

How can a woman submit to her husband when he has not taken up his position as head of the home?

"¹Wives, likewise, be submissive to your own husbands, that even if some do not obey the word, they, without a word, may be won by the conduct of their wives."
1 Peter 3.1

The word **conduct** means the act, manner, or process of carrying on. It also means a mode or standard of personal behavior, especially as based on moral principles.

The more a woman tries to change her husband with words, the worse the situation will become because the words will hit like a ton of bricks on his "ego" and this is something that no man can accept.

Ladies, never try to change your husband by yourself. Stop trying to convert him. Don't be his personal Pastor by leaving sermon tapes or messages every where he goes. Instead, you should shock him with your submission and by becoming his ideal helper. Your changed attitude will make your husband say, "Oh! What happened to you?" Make him say, "Wow! Something is different about you."

3. The wife should respect her husband

"³³Nevertheless let each one of you in particular so love his own wife as himself, and let the wife see that she respects her husband." Ephesians 5.33

Respect goes hand in hand with submission. If the woman is having a hard time submitting to her husband, then she will have an even harder time respecting him. Respect for a husband has nothing to do with his personal success, but in his position as husband.

Respect means to yield to someone his proper position. The worse way a wife can be disrespectful to her husband is by the words of her mouth.

How do you respect or yield to your husband and his position in the family?

- When you don't tell him to be quiet or disrespect him in public. To win him over without words means that you will not preach to him all the time concerning the things that he needs to do. Men really hate to be told or reminded what they need to do because it hurts their "ego". Change your strategy.

- When your husband disciplines your children, you should support and endorse his word and his authority. If you don't support him in front of your children, you are rejecting and taking away his authority in the home; this is extremely disrespectful.

- When you allow him to have the last word and make the final decision. You can make suggestions regarding a specific situation, but the final decision should always be his. Back him up; allow him to feel that he is truly the man and the head of his family.

4. Woman was created to reproduce

God created woman with the great responsibility to reproduce the seed. The woman is like an incubator;

her job is to reproduce everything that her husband puts in her hand.

5. To fulfill her husband sexually

The Word of God teaches that the woman should not deny herself sexually to her husband; otherwise, she opens the door for the enemy to come in and destroy their marriage. This is a major problem in today's society. Women deny themselves to their husbands and as a result the husband is tempted to look at other women, which eventually leads to infidelity and adultery. Sometimes the woman is at fault be-cause she must fulfill her marital responsibility at all times. For the sake of argument, let us say that the woman is less sexually active than the man is, this still doesn't give her the right to deny herself to her husband; this is a sin.

Why should you never deny yourself sexually to your spouse?

• Because denying yourself leads to temptation.

> "⁵Do not deprive one another except with consent for a time, that you may give yourselves to fasting and prayer; and come together again so that Satan does not tempt you because of your lack of self-control."
> 1 Corinthians 7.5

- You open doors to adultery and infidelity.

- Because it is a sin.

When the man assumes the responsibility as leader and spiritual priest in the home, the woman will always support and follow him with respect, and so on. Therefore, it is safe to say that the man is directly or indirectly responsible for the success or failure of the marriage. The man should always be the one who initiates the fulfillment of his roles and functions in the home. When the woman sees her husband take over his role as the head of the home, then she will willingly and joyfully do her corresponding part.

CHAPTER 5

Communication in the Home

"So then, my beloved brethren, let every man be swift to hear, slow to speak, slow to wrath."
James 1.19

When we surveyed couples about their marital problems the most common answer that made its way to the top was the lack of communication. By nature, the man is less communicative than the woman. His lack of communication creates major division in the relationship. In this chapter, we will be discussing the different levels of communication and how to identify ourselves in this area.

Three levels of communication in the home

1. **Conversational.** This type of conversation is a quick exchange of words such as in a greeting or a goodbye. We practice this mode of conversation most of the time and it doesn't require a personal relationship.

2. **Communicate and convey small details**. This type of communication goes beyond the hello and

good-bye words. Time is taken to engage in small talk that can range from daily events, to information regarding the things that need to be done during the day or perhaps something that is happening at home and with our families. The things we share at this time are not deep thoughts or emotions, but rather informal information. There is no need for a personal relationship when we discuss simple events in our lives. For instance, when we share, in detail, how the church service was, what the day at the job was like, comments on a sport's event, the trip to the supermarket, etc.

3. **Communicating intimate and personal things.** At this level of communication, people and couples, share very deep, personal intimacies, feelings, emotions and painful events. Detailed emotions and feelings are expressed concerning visions, spiritual experiences, personal encounters with God, and more. This is the highest level of communication that can be shared between two people. Unfortunately, many couples never graduate to the second level before the fight breaks out and the verbal confrontation begins. Once this happens, frustration takes over opening the door for divorce because neither side is willing or able to properly channel his or her emotions in a way that they can be heard and understood. To reach

this level of communication, a personal relationship must be present.

Sometimes the spoken word hurts more than the action.

"¹A soft answer turns away wrath, but a harsh word stirs up anger." Proverbs 15.1

We must understand the power behind the words that we speak to begin to establish a solid and positive communication with our family. Many times people are deeply hurt, not by what is done to them, but by the words that were spoken against them. The Word of God commands the woman to build her home with the words of her mouth. Women have the power to build or destroy with her words. Because a woman speaks more words than a man does, she must be extremely careful of what she says.

"¹The wise woman builds her house, but the foolish pulls it down with her hands." Proverbs 14.1

The reason communication is lost in the home is because respect has also been lost.

How can you have effective communication in your home with your spouse and children?

1. You must learn to listen

"19 So then, my beloved brethren, let every man be swift to hear, slow to speak, slow to wrath." James 1.19

Listening is a learned art. Many people suffer from deafness, which has created a shortage of listeners in the world today. We have to learn to listen before we open our mouths to speak.

"13He who answers a matter before he hears it, it is folly and shame to him." Proverbs 18.13

On the average, most people are only able to achieve a few seconds of listening time.

When we learn to listen we learn to:

- **Understand people.** The Lord said that from the abundance of the heart the mouth speaks. When we are good listeners, we are able to know and understand what is hidden in the heart of men. Obedience consists in finding the true nature of things. Therefore, when we learn to listen to people, we are able to identify the root or nature of their problems.

- **Minister and council people.** When we become good listeners, we are better able to discern the nature of people's problems. Knowing this, we are better able to minister and give words of godly advice, giving them comfort and guidance. God will always give us the right word to say which will satisfy the needs of the people.

- **Lighten the load.** The simple act of listening will lighten the burden of the person talking to us. He or she will feel relieved once they unload their burden, guilt, hurt feelings, internal pressure, peer pressure, or anything else that might be on their minds.

When we find someone who willingly takes the time to really listen, it means that we have found the greatest treasure in life.

We must force ourselves to learn how to listen to people. One thing we must remember when we listen to people is to hear what they say and look at the situation from their perspective. When someone is talking to you, don't interrupt because this blocks the communication process. Remember that when you listen, you are doing your spouse, your children and the people around you a favor. Sometimes, the only thing our children want is for mommy and daddy to listen to them. Take advantage of the special moment when your spouse or children want to talk to you, really listen to them. If you wait for another time when you "feel" like talking, more than likely you will miss the opportunity to do so because they will no longer want to do it.

2. Speak the truth

The Lord said, *"But let your 'Yes' be 'Yes,' and your 'No,' 'No,' lest you fall into judgment."* Your honesty and transparency will keep you safe from getting hurt in the future. The truth will always prevail and when it is said in love, it might hurt for a moment, but later it will heal the broken heart.

3. Learning your spouse's and children's love language

One virtue of "agape" love is that it is unselfish; it doesn't seek to be self-gratifying. Real love is demonstrated when you strive to learn your family's love language. What is a love language? Love language is nothing more than the likes and dislikes of your spouse and children, what makes them happy, what they need to feel loved. Once you understand what their love language is, you should do everything in your power to make them happy.

There are five love languages and these are the same for the men, women and children:

- **Words of affirmation**. People need to be affirmed in every area of their life: in their emotions, mental stability and spirituality. People need affirmation when they do something right, and when they make mistakes, they need words of encouragement. A good leader will always affirm his employees or the people under his authority with words that assure, encourage and motivate them, either in the good job they are doing, their service for the ministry and in their personal identity; don't criticize.

- **Physical touch.** Physical contact is one way to communicate love to your family. Children, who are held in your arms for a period of time, and who are embraced and hugged, are often more emotionally stable than the children who go for a long time without any physical contact. Play with them or practice their favorite sport. The important thing is for you to have physical contact with them. These can't be absent in the home.

- **Acts of service.** Doing things that you know your family loves you to do for them. For instance, cook, serve the table, wash the dishes, take out the garbage or just help out in any way you can. When you make the effort to serve your family, they will feel appreciated and loved.

- **Quality time.** One love language which the family always demands, specially the spouse and children, is quality time.

- **Gifts.** Gifts demonstrate our love and appreciation towards the people in our lives. These gifts should be carefully selected according to the wants and needs of the individual, prior to giving them out. However, the most important aspect of this love language is to recognize it and to be willing to supply this need.

You achieve great communication and close relationships with your family during quality time.

Example of quality time spent with your family:

- Take a vacation once a year.
- Allow time in your busy schedule to play with your children.
- Take time to talk about the things that are most important such as your relationship, marriage, children, church, etc. (make sure the TV is off).
- Separate a weekend and spend time with your spouse, alone (dedicate the entire time to your spouse).

What is your spouse's love language? Once you know and understand what your spouse's love language is, you will improve your relationship and communication in your home.

The foundation of a great ministry is the family unit, but if your family is not in the best of shape right now, your ministry will suffer. I strongly believe that the best way to restore the communication in the home is to ask your spouse for forgiveness if you have been disrespectful. Let us begin to establish solid relationships, beginning with quality time.

CHAPTER 6

Sex in Marriage

Sex in marriage

It is taboo to talk about sex in churches, the home or with your spouse and children today. Many marriages end up in divorce because of sex, or lack of it.

"⁶My people are destroyed for lack of knowledge. Because you have rejected knowledge, I also will reject you from being priest for Me; because you have forgotten the law of your God, I also will forget your children." Hosea 4.6

Unity in a marriage exists on three levels: Spirit, soul (will, emotions and intellect), and body, with sex being a major part of this union.

What is the purpose of sex in marriage?

- **To procreate.** God commanded man to go out and multiply.

- **For pleasure.** God created sex for men and women to enjoy each other within the blessing of marriage. Unfortunately, the enemy has made it his job to distort everything that has to do with sex in order to destroy God's plans.

"18May your fountain be blessed, and may you rejoice in the wife of your youth." Proverbs 5.18

Why couples have a hard time enjoying sex and intimacy

- **Sexual abuse.** Many people have lived through painful sexual abuse and as a result they consider sex to be something terrible and disgusting. These people are unable to enjoy sex with their spouse.

- **Taboo about sex.** Any taboo that has to do with sex is the devil's lie. For instance, some people are taught that sex is only for procreation and not for enjoyment. The truth is that sex within marriage is beautiful and pure; this is how God created it.

- **Selfish partners.** This is a common problem in couples, especially in men. During sexual intimacy, the man seeks his own pleasure without any regard for his wife's sexual satisfaction.

- **The woman needs more time to reach her sexual orgasm.** Every man needs to understand this: the woman achieves her orgasm when she is treated with love, tenderness and gentle caressing; she can't be rushed and this takes time and patience.

- **Man is quicker when it comes to ejaculation.** By nature, the man has no problem enjoying sex or achieving ejaculation. However, the woman takes a lot longer to be satisfied because this is the way that God created her.

Women need the following ingredients to be fulfilled and to experience sexual satisfaction:

- **Security.** The only one who can provide security for a woman is the husband when he is fulfilling his position as the head or leader of the home. When the wife feels insecure, it reflects in intimacy.

- **Love (she needs to feel loved).** The husband provides this feeling of being loved when he is fully active as the emotional provider in the home. If the husband is not verbally, emotionally or physically loving to his wife, then she is not going to respond in a positive way.

- **The ability to express emotion.** Communication is the door that allows emotions to be expressed. If the wife is going to bed burdened by the many situations going on around her, she will not be able to enjoy sexual intimacy. She needs to have time to unload her frustrations and anxieties with her husband by talking things out.

- **The ability to express herself.** It is the woman's nature to want to express the way she feels in detail. When the husband listens patiently to whatever she has to say, then she will be a willing participant when it comes to sexual intimacy.

- **Communication.** Husbands need to be good listeners because wives need to be heard by them.

- **She needs to feel beautiful.** Women need to hear that they are special and beautiful, especially from their husbands.

- **Words of affirmation.** A woman needs to hear words of affirmation everyday, letting her know that she is appreciated and important.

- **She needs to feel needed.** Men need to convey to their wives that they are needed with beautiful words of affirmation.

These ingredients need to be present in a woman's life for her to feel sexually satisfied; men were created to satisfy the woman's every need.

Which sexual aberrations are prohibited in the Bible and should never be practiced in marriage?

God instituted sanitary, sexual and health laws for His people. The Jewish people were to follow these laws. God has also given us laws, parameters and limitations that need to be kept in marriage and outside of it.

What is an aberration? Everything that goes against nature and the way God created it. In other words, everything that is anti-natural.

"21And you shall not let any of your descendants pass through the fire to Molech, nor shall you profane the name of your God: I am the LORD. 22You shall not lie with a male as with a woman. It is an abomination. 23Nor shall you mate with any animal, to defile yourself with it. Nor shall any woman stand before an animal to mate with it. It is perversion. 24"Do not defile yourselves with any of these things; for by all these the nations are defiled, which I am casting out before you." Leviticus 18.21-24

A few of the most common aberrations are:

Incest	Masochism
Adultery	Exhibitionism
Masturbation	Voyeurism
Homosexuality	Transvestite
Bestiality	Transsexual

105

Paganism	Necrophilia
Pornography	Prostitution
Sadism	Rape

These and many more like it are contrary to God's creation, and if these are practiced, curse and destruction will come into the marriage.

CHAPTER 7

Separation and Divorce

$\mathcal{M}$any people are still suffering the catastrophic consequences of divorce while others are still experiencing great emotional turmoil remembering the process.

What is a divorce?

The word **divorce** translated from the Greek language literally means to **abandon**, meaning to relinquish your position without permission. Divorce also means to divert, to leave one's husband, the action or instance of legally dissolving a marriage. When two people unite together in the bond of matrimony, they become as one flesh. When they choose divorce as a way out of the marriage covenant, they are doing it without permission because in God's eyes, marriage is an irrevocable covenant or pact.

Divorce is like a soldier who says, "I hate being a soldier, I want to be a regular citizen again."

The subject of divorce has brought about much controversy, condemnation and guilt to the Christian people. To better understand this subject clearly and in line with the Word of God, we need to consider the following principles of interpretation.

Principles of interpretation:

- When interpreting the Word, you must think of something literal concerning the subject you are reading about.
- You must research the historical background of the verse that you are reading.
- You must read the verses before and after the one you are meditating on.

Where does divorce come from?

Divorce started with the law during Moses' time.

"⁷They said to Him, "Why then did Moses command to give a certificate of divorce, and to put her away?" ⁸He said to them, "Moses, because of the hardness of your hearts, permitted you to divorce your wives, but from the beginning it was not so." Matthew 19.7, 8

What does *"hardness of heart"* mean? It means that because of their stubborn hearts, they were led to commit adultery. What excuse or reason did Moses allow the people to use when they wanted a divorce? Moses doesn't consent adultery to be used as a condition for divorce because this sin already had death by stoning as punishment. During the days of Moses, there was no basis for divorce. However, men started to complain and leave their wives for insignificant reasons. Because of what happened during this time, when Jesus came along, the Pharisees asked Him if it was lawful for a man to disown and divorce his wife for any reason. Before answering this question, you have to remember that Moses was protecting the women of his day by forcing the men to do the following:

- Write a paper of divorce.
- Give her a divorce.
- Let her go. (This meant that men had to leave their wives with money and material wealth).

The Pharisees were letting the women go empty-handed and with the warning that they could never re-marry.

Jesus said that Moses gave his ancestors their divorce papers because their hearts were hardened and to protect the women from being left empty-handed, in poverty and misery, indigent and without hope of ever finding someone else to marry. Jesus said that they could not disown or divorce their wives under any circumstance. Furthermore, He said that He had come to bring mercy, and instead of stoning a woman to death because she was caught in the sin of adultery, it was better to grant her a divorce. Adultery is the only accepted grounds for divorce.

God hates divorce, but He loves those who are divorced.

Some people have the mistaken idea that divorce is the unpardonable sin. They label a divorcee as someone whose sin is unforgivable. But the blood of Jesus is bigger, greater and more powerful than any divorce. In the Old Testament, wives were not allowed to divorce their husbands because they were considered the man's property, like a house, land or an animal. But Jesus said that He was changing this because He came to completely redeem women that they might be able to enjoy the same rights as men.

"12And if a woman divorces her husband and marries another, she commits adultery." Mark 10.12

Traumas caused by separation and divorce

Many things happen when a couple decides to get a divorce. There are also terrible consequences when the marriage covenant is broken. For instance:

- A broken spirit
- A shattered and crushed spirit

- A hurting soul

A person with a **broken spirit** feels like his world is spinning out of control and wants desperately to stop the pain. He doesn't have the desire to work; his dreams are shuttered; he has no motivation. But there is hope; Jesus came with an anointing to heal the broken-hearted.

Never make the mistake of confusing who you are with what you have done. Don't confuse a mistake for failure. Perhaps you do something wrong today, but this mistake doesn't mean that you are a failure. Never measure your personal worth by the mistakes that you make because it is only human to be im- perfect, and imperfect people make mistakes. If it was your intention to do something right the first time and it didn't work out, don't worry about it, in God there are always second chances. If you have been hurt don't give up. Make a decision to start again with God; He is your helper. Measure your personal worth knowing that it was God who created you and made you worthy, before you made any mistakes, and before that person that you now call your spouse, walked into your life. The blood of Jesus is powerful enough to cleanse all evil-doing when we repent wholeheartedly, and in Jesus, there is always a second chance.

What is the Biblical reason for divorce according to Jesus?

- **Adultery and fornication**. It is noteworthy to understand that adultery and fornication are the only Biblical foundations for divorce. But, as always, there are other very specific and special circumstances that must be dealt with carefully before considering these as legal basis for a divorce. Regardless of what the situation is, we must always seek the Holy Spirit for guidance.

CHAPTER 8

Single and Satisfied

It seems like the church has classified single adults as second class citizens. There are many people out there living alone and frustrated because they want to find someone special to be married to. There are also people who are now married who spend too much time thinking about getting a divorce. These people are not content with their relationships or the way their lives are going, and all they can think about is how they can change their living status.

You might say, "Pastor, you just don't understand what I am going through. You don't know what it's like to be single and alone." Two men in the Bible give us the answer to this dilemma, Jesus and Paul.

Allow me to share with you two principles which single people should follow.

"24Brethren, let each one remain with God in that state in which he was called. 25 Now concerning virgins: I have no commandment from the Lord; yet I give judgment as one whom the Lord in His mercy has made trustworthy. 26I

suppose therefore that this is good because of the present distress--that it is good for a man to remain as he is: [27] Are you bound to a wife? Do not seek to be loosed. Are you loosed from a wife? Do not seek a wife. [28] But even if you do marry, you have not sinned; and if a virgin marries, she has not sinned. Nevertheless such will have trouble in the flesh, but I would spare you." 1 Corinthians 7.24-28

Now we will analyze these verses in more detail. There are a few noteworthy key words or phrases:

- **Remain with God.** Perhaps this phrase doesn't sound very deep, but it does make us reflect on the people who are waiting for something or someone to stroll into their lives instead of waiting on God to improve their lives. There is a big difference between making time and purposely waiting on God. If you are truly waiting right now, then you should be serving God as you strive to strengthen your personal relationship with Him.

- **"... in that state in which he was called."** Paul referred to the civil status of a person, whether married or single, to a "calling". Your calling is directly related to your civil status. The day that Jesus came into your heart, God established your calling. Therefore, the day that you decide to get married, you better be sure that you are marrying the right person at the right time. Otherwise, a decision made in haste can deeply affect the purpose, will and calling of God for your life. Now that you are in Christ, your first priority is not your civil status, but finding out what your calling and purpose is for your life in God.

For instance, many people are looking for ways to change their lives because they have a deep need to feel worthy or to find meaning to their existence. Instead, they should be concentrating on finding out what their purpose is, and what their calling is in God; this is the only thing that will bring true meaning to life. Why are so many people still single? Because they are not waiting on God, they are waiting for a person. If you are waiting for the "perfect" person to walk into your life and change your sadness into happiness, or your loneliness into companionship, then you are placing yourself in the perfect position to be hurt. Wait on God; He will never let you down.

How do you wait on God? You need to keep busy finding out what your calling is and fulfilling it; you must be serving Christ. If you choose to wait on God, you are going to need His help, but you will not receive it if you're living in sin or if you are in covenant with the world. For instance, God can't help you, or bring you together with the person that He has in mind for you, if your life is not in order.

Wrong reasons to begin a relationship or to get married

- **Because you feel alone.** I am a witness to many people who are now married yet still feel alone even when they are "together". They sleep in separate rooms and live separate lives. The answer to loneliness in not found in a human being, it is found in God; He is the only one who can fill the emptiness in your heart.

"¹⁰I have seen the God-given task with which the sons of men are to be occupied." Ecclesiastes 3.10

- **Because you want to improve your financial status.** When you get married, the expenses increase because you are no longer one, but two. Never make the decision to get married because you need or want to increase your financial holdings; you will be making a terrible mistake.

- **Unrestrained sexual desires.** Serving God and concentrating on your calling will help you to stay focused and control yourself and your sexual urges. I strongly believe that many people decide to get married because their hormones are out of control; they have not learned how to control them with the help of the Holy Spirit.

- **To get away from the parents or just to leave home.** In 1 Corinthians 7.27 it says, *"Are you loosed from a wife? Do not seek a wife."* The same thing can be said to single people. Stop looking for a spouse. You might ask, "How am I going to find someone special to spend the rest of my life with?" The same way that God did it. He put Adam to sleep, opened up His side and removed a rib, closed him up and created Eve. In other words, Adam didn't say, "I am twenty-five years old and I need a wife." God made the decision that he should not be alone and thus, Eve was created. God is the perfect matchmaker. He knows where to find your Adam or Eve. If you really want to find a husband or wife, then allow God to bring him or her to you. He is the only one who knows where, and who, your ideal helper is. It is obvious that you have no idea where your ideal partner is, otherwise, you would be married already.

Young people and adults are frustrated because they are having a hard time finding Mr. Right or Mrs. Right. You might be dating someone and say, "Yes, he/she is the right one!" But without knowing it, you might be further from the truth than you think. Stop looking for a partner and concentrate on developing your calling and service to God, He will introduce you to the right person, at the right time. You have no need to go out to clubs, single's meetings, worldly parties or bars to find your soul mate. It is not Biblical to pretend that you can find the right person by dating many people for short periods of time. This only leads to disaster.

Pastor what should I do to find somebody?

- Keep your attention on God. If you concentrate on Him, you will realize that it is unnecessary to be dating all time to find the right person. Wait for the Holy Spirit's signal, He will tell you who the right person is. Feel confident that the Holy Spirit knows what He is doing. Isaac met Rebecca one day and married her the following day. He knew she was the right person for him because he was connected to God.

  Ruth and Boaz are another example of two people who found each other as they went about doing the right thing.

  "28But even if you do marry, you have not sinned; and if a virgin marries, she has not sinned. Nevertheless such will have trouble in the flesh, but I would spare you." 1 Corinthians 7.28

Marriage implies difficulty, according to the verse you just read. Marriage doesn't solve problems, but it is an opportunity to share the best of who we are with someone else. If you're single and feeling lonely and miserable, then allow me to inform you that marriage will only make matters worse. The marriage covenant should be taken seriously and for the right reasons, otherwise, it is a disaster before it even begins. Marriage is not an escape route from your problems, but rather, it is a commitment that you willingly make with another person and with God. Why don't you ask a few married people if they would get married again if they had the chance? Their answer would probably be "no" because of the many problems and conflicts that they are experiencing. I have two very interesting questions to ask you: "Are you willing to face the conflicts and difficulties, which are normal within marriage, wholeheartedly, and without giving up?" Why do you want to get married?"

Illustration: A couple is talking. Another couple watches them with curiosity and wonder. The on-lookers make the comment, "What a happy couple." However, that "happy" couple is thinking the same about the spectators. This is a very common assumption to make because what we see from the outside is not always the true representation of what is really going on.

It is worth waiting for the right person to come along instead of spending the rest of your life with the wrong person.

- **"Wait on God"**

The amplified Bible says, *"[29]I mean, brethren, the appointed time has been winding down and it has grown very short. From now on, let even those who have wives be as if they had none."* 1 Corinthians 7.29

God changes the perspective on things and says that *"even those who have wives be as if they had none"* because marriage doesn't exist in eternity; it ends when we die. We need to keep our eyes fixed on eternity and not on natural, perishable things. God has a plan for your life, as long as you remain single. But, if you spend all of your free time thinking about your future wedding and the person who will become your spouse, then you will be wasting time that could be better spent fulfilling God's purpose and calling for your life.

For instance, God says, "After Maria finishes what she started for the edification of my kingdom, then I will grant her the desire of her heart, I will give her a husband." But Maria is so busy doing other things, within which is the task of finding a husband. She spends too much time wondering who her future husband is and what he looks like. She even plans her wedding down to the smallest detail. Her time is consumed in dreams and neglects to do what God entrusted her to accomplish. God is not going to give Maria her ideal helper until she finishes what He has asked her to do. Time is too short to be wasted on things like a future marriage, money, pleasures, etc.

- **"Single people take care of God's business."**

The amplified Bible says, *"[32]My desire is to have you free from all anxiety and distressing care. The unmarried man is anxious about the things of the Lord--how he may please the Lord." 1 Corinthians 7.32*

There are many people today feeling frustrated and miserable because they have yet to understand why God wants them to be single. The only time you should really worry about getting married is during your private prayer time. At any other time, God receives this as a sin.

"[6]Be anxious for nothing, but in everything by prayer and supplication, with thanksgiving, let your requests be made known to God." Philippians 4.6

You might say, "Lord, I surrender all of my anxiety to you. I believe and trust in you. I know that you have the right person for me and that at the right time you will bring her or him into my life. In the meantime, I will serve and honor you." Why is God keeping you single? What is He doing in you, for you, and upon you that can only be accomplished while you are single? Why can't you do it when you get married? If you are unable to answer these questions then you are not ready for God to send you a husband or wife.

If God says that you should wait ten years for your husband or wife, then He is not going to bring them into your life until this time is fulfilled. There is nothing you can do to change this.

Illustration: Some people might say, "I am praying and waiting, but time is slowly passing by and I feel frustrated." This is the same as thinking about the end of the workday before it even begins; it makes the day feel endless. If you concentrate on everything that you have to do at work, then the hours will pass by quickly and the end of the day will come before you know it. If you waste your time watching the clock, your workday will seem endless. You might even wonder if the clock is on a break. The fact is that the clock will seem to move faster or slower depending on how much effort you are placing on your service for the kingdom. If you want the ten years to pass by quickly, begin to serve today and I can assure you that they will be gone before you know it.

- **"Marriage in God is forever."**

Once you enter into the marriage covenant, there is no way out. "But I didn't know it was going to be like this!" I'm sorry, you made a commitment and there is no way out of it. "Yes, but she snores!" I'm sorry, you made a commitment and there is no way out of it. "He is not gentle or caring!" There is no way out. People should really learn to enjoy their years as single people because once they get married, there is no way out. As single people, you can go anywhere you want, get home at the time you choose, eat what your heart desires, dress anyway you want, but in marriage, this all changes. The disciples understood what Jesus was saying, that it was better to be alone because while you wait, you will become a successful man or woman of God.

Being Christian doesn't mean that you have to look homely or unattractive. You shouldn't say, "If I were married, I would lose weight!" But why wait, lose weight now and someone will notice you. There are also very "spiritual" and good-looking men that are under the mistaken impression that their pleasant features give them rights to date every woman who crosses their path. I have news for you, "You are not God's gift to women!" The only person you should date is the man or woman of God, who will be your spouse.

Joseph did not compromise his principles. There is a saying that goes, "The pilot postpones landing the plane when he perceives danger." Well, God is holding you back from getting married because he has a purpose for your life by keeping you single a while longer. God sees you as a single pilot. Wait for the danger to pass before landing a wife or husband.

"[46]Joseph was thirty years old when he stood before Pharaoh king of Egypt. And Joseph went out from the presence of Pharaoh, and went throughout all the land of Egypt." Genesis 41.46

God works in your life and character as you serve, honor and fulfill your calling. He takes care of the rest, including finding your spouse. Don't get married for the wrong reasons. Ask God for direction. Remember God is keeping you single for a reason!

CHAPTER 9

Children

*C*urses and blessings are passed down from generation to generation. As parents, our deepest desire should be to build strong generations.

"¹Praise the LORD! Blessed is the man who fears the LORD, who delights greatly in His commandments. ²His descendants will be mighty on earth; the generation of the upright will be blessed. ³Wealth and riches will be in his house, and his righteousness endures forever. ⁴Unto the upright there arises light in the darkness; He is gracious, and full of compassion, and righteous. ⁵A good man deals graciously and lends; he will guide his affairs with discretion. ⁶Surely he will never be shaken; the righteous will be in everlasting remembrance." Psalms 112.1-6

"⁷…keeping mercy for thousands, forgiving iniquity and transgression and sin, by no means clearing the guilty, visiting the iniquity of the fathers upon the children and the children's children to the third and the fourth generation." Exodus 34.7

What is the best method for raising our children?

"⁶Train up a child in the way he should go, and when he is old he will not depart from it." Proverbs 22.6

Instruction. The word **"instruction"** in Hebrew is the word *"chanar,"* meaning to imitate, teach, dedicate, consecrate, instruct and discipline. As parents, we are called to instruct, guide and discipline our children.

What mistakes are parents making when disciplining their children?

"⁴And you, fathers, do not provoke your children to wrath, but bring them up in the training and admonition of the Lord." Ephesians 6.4

"²¹Fathers, do not provoke your children, lest they become discouraged." Colossians 3.21

Sometimes parents provoke their children to wrath or anger. They exasperate their children into doing things they don't like to do. They corner and mistreat them. This negative attitude towards their children, during puberty and adolescence, wounds their spirit. Let us learn the attitudes that parents have towards their children and how they respond to it.

Parents Attitudes	The Child's Response	Result
• Strong language	• Anger	• Wounded spirit
• Unfair punishment	• Low self-esteem	• Feeling unworthy
• Broken promises	• Deception	• Sadness
• Absence of verbal affirmation	• Rejection	• Insecurity and fear
• Favoritism towards another sibling	• Self-rejection	• Jealousy among the sibling

What is the evidence that a child is hurting?

- Lack of communication
- Ungrateful
- Stubborn
- Passive rebellious attitude
- Aggressive rebellious attitude
- Self-justifying
- Depression
- Attention grabber

The main reason why children are rebellious during puberty and adolescence is because they are hurting inside.

The solution to a child who has a wounded spirit is inner healing and deliverance.

Damaging attitudes of parents against their children, which can hurt them emotionally

- **Perfectionism** – When too much is expected of them, when expectations are beyond the norm. The father who demands perfection is obsessive and wants everything to be perfect; this attitude damages the heart and mind of a child.

- **Over protective** – When parents are obsessive and controlling, the children are not allowed to make decisions for themselves. These children grow up feeling rejected and rebellious.

- **Excessively indulgent** – Too many gifts and rewards are given to the child to compensate for physical and verbal love. This child will have an abundance of material things he does not need and be lacking in what is truly important, love, and as a result, he feels hurt and wounded.

- **Hypochondriac** – Parents who neglect to give enough attention and love to their children will raise them up to become attention grabbers by constantly complaining of being sick or feeling pain, exaggerating any sign of illness.

- **Rejection** – Some children are rejected from the beginning when they were in their mother's womb, and as a result, they grow up with emotional problems; everything they do is rejected by their parents and peers.

Different methods of discipline:

- **Lack of discipline.** This is the cruelest way to raise up a child. He grows up learning how to do things the hard way because he was never taught how to do it right at home. A child that grows up without discipline feels a sense of detachment from the family. In other words, he doesn't feel like part of the family. The Bible says that a child, who is not disciplined, is a bastard.

"⁸Now if you are exempt from correction and left without discipline in which all [of God's children] share, then you are illegitimate offspring and not true sons [at all]." Hebrews 12.8 (Amplified Bible)

- **Excessive discipline:** Physical abuse makes the child feel rejected and fearful towards authority figures. Some parents punish their children in inhumane and brutal ways.

"¹⁸Discipline your son while there is hope, but do not [indulge your angry resentments by undue chastisements and] set yourself to his ruin." Proverbs 19.18 (Amplified Bible)

- **Not enforcing the punishment.** When parents warn their children of impending punishment, but never follow through, they lose their children's respect. I am about to give you the most important advice you will ever receive on raising children, never go against your spouse's authority or punishment for your children, especially in front of the children. This will result in terrible conflicts in the home and with your children.

How should you discipline your children?

There are three levels of discipline:

1. The first level is instruction. You must instruct and set guidelines for your children on how to behave or act before you discipline them for doing it wrong.

"⁶Train up a child in the way he should go, and when he is old he will not depart from it." Proverbs 22.6

We can't expect our children to behave a certain way unless we teach them right from wrong and good from bad.

Two ways to give instruction:

By our own example, being a worthy role model and by teaching proper behavior through:

- **Correction:** It is the parent's responsibility to correct, but God has the last word on authority.

- **Teach the child** right from wrong before applying discipline and punishment. Ask yourself, "Did I ever say to him not to do that?" It is important for the child to understand why he is being punished or he will get hurt and resent his parents.

Teach the child in the following areas:

- **Obedience.** You need to teach your children to respect and obey authority.

- **Respect.** When your children misbehave, it is your job to teach them respect.

- **Responsibility.** You should teach them at an early age to have certain responsibilities at home.

Teaching establishes the guidelines for proper behavior, thoughts and attitudes that will govern their actions later on in life. It is extremely important for parents to recognize their children's character.

2. The second level of discipline is "the warning". The first thing you should ask yourself when the child disobeys is, "Were my instructions clear?" If you feel that your instructions were not clear, then teach them

137

again. "Was his reaction against my authority or did he simply forget?" "Was he being forward with me?" "Did I hurt his feelings or wound his spirit in any way that caused him to be angry with me?" "Should I ask forgiveness for something that I did wrong?"

3. The third level of discipline is "correction". Teach your child to be accountable for his actions. Ask him, "Did you do this?" Never punish him in public. The father should always discipline his child, but in his absence, the mother should do it.

What type of punishment should be enforced?

- **Emotional discipline.** This is not the time to make the child feel guilty for his mistake but rather appeal to his conscious allowing God to deal with him. For instance, "James, it is disrespectful to answer back to the people. God doesn't like that."

- **Physical discipline.** The Word of God teaches that a child should be disciplined with the rod. Never punish your child in anger. Punishment executed in love, even when the rod is used, will always bring positive results.

"[13]Do not withhold correction from a child, for if you beat him with a rod, he will not die." Proverbs 23.13

"¹⁸Chasten your son while there is hope, and do not set your heart on his destruction." Proverbs 19.18

- **Mental discipline.** This discipline is the removal of your child's favorite things to do. For instance, sports, television, sharing with friends, etc.

Begin teaching and disciplining your children so that they will grow up and become healthy, responsible adults, instead of difficult and weak people that will burden our families and us. Parents begin to discipline your children, correct and instruct them in line with God's Word, which says:

"²⁴He who spares his rod hates his son, but he who loves him disciplines him promptly." Proverbs 13.24

Prayer of Repentance

*R*ight now, where you are sitting, if you desire to receive the greatest gift of eternal life through Jesus Christ, then read the following prayer out loud:

"Heavenly Father, I recognize that I am a sinner and that my sin separates me from you. I repent from all of my sins and confess Jesus as my Lord and Savior, of my own free will. I believe He died for my sins. I believe with all my heart that God, the Father, raised Him from the dead. Jesus, I ask you to come into my heart and change my life. I renounce all covenants with the enemy. If I die right now, when I open my eyes, I will be in your arms. Amen!

If this prayer reflects the sincere desire of your heart, observe what Jesus said about the decision you just made:

"9If you confess with your mouth the Lord Jesus and believe in your heart that God has raised Him from the dead, you will be saved. 10For with the heart one believes unto righteousness, and with the mouth confession is made unto salvation." Romans 10.9, 10

"47Most assuredly, I say to you, he who believes in Me has everlasting life." John 6.47

Conclusion

"*Through wisdom a house is built, and by understanding it is established.*"
Proverbs 24.3

It is my prayer before God, that in reading or studying this book, you were edified by its teachings on the marriage covenant. Also, that you learned how to teach and discipline your children and that you understand that you have the ability to deliver your children from the bondage of slavery and calamity, which many times are inherited. In Christ Jesus, Amen!

Testimonies

Raul and Lourdes Botana

We were married at a very young age in 1968. During the last thirty years of marriage, we have experienced terrible moments of crisis and demands, accusations of guilt and endless wait for the other to fill the emptiness we felt in our lives. For ten years we were active in our church holding positions of leadership, and after endless marriage counseling sessions with different professionals, our problems seemed hopeless. For short periods of time, things would stabilize and times were good, but we continued to go from one crisis to another. Little by little, we started to drift apart emotionally and spiritually. A feeling of hopelessness grew in our relationship and we were no longer able to understand each other's needs. We started to concentrate on each other's weaknesses instead of our virtues. Instead of taking responsibility for our behavior, and trying to work things out, we felt like victims. We started to believe that our situation had no solution and that we were wasting each other's time. My husband stopped attending church and I became bitter towards him for not being the spiritual leader that I expected him to be. I felt misunderstood, controlled and verbally abused. On the other hand, he felt that I didn't respect him and that I considered myself superior to him. Also, we had our daily dose of financial struggles, raising the children and daily situations, but as for me, I felt emotionally drained and empty of my husband's attention. He felt I wasn't supportive enough and that all I could think about was my own needs and wants.

One day, early in the morning, we had a terrible discussion, which ended in him leaving home. I did not call him or ask him to come back. After several weeks, he signed the divorce papers. This was shocking to me because I never expected him to make this decision, even though we were going through such rough moments. We were at the time of our lives when our children were already grown, and after thirty years of marriage, this was happening to us; it was an eye opening experience! Slowly, I started feel anger towards my husband for doing this. The anger and wrath that I felt was the emotion kept me going. It justified my actions and made me declare that perhaps this was the right thing to do. But as time passed, after three years of divorce, when the anger wasted away, I was able to realize that now I had a broken home and that our dreams and aspirations had disappeared. I had suffered the loss of the family unit and everything that comes with it, the pain, joy, shared moments and the love we shared. Our family and children were affected greatly. This was a sad situation. Through it all, I continued in my profession and Raul in his business. We were living separate and independent lives. Two years after our divorce, I started to shine as an independent woman, completely separated from Raul; he was living like a playboy.

One day, a friend came and invited me to her church, which she really loved. I agreed because I really wanted to fellowship again and to restore my Christian life. I knew it was the only answer. The day I visited El Rey Jesus Church, which at the time was located in a very small building, and where the people were packed in like sardines, I said, "Oh, Lord, I can't do this!" After a few moments inside the church, I heard a voice speak inside of me saying, "Give this a chance." I agreed and started to attend every Sunday. Little by little, my outlook on this small church started to change and I started to join in the festivity and to understand that this was the church God wanted me to participate in. After several months, I heard Pastora Ana Maldonado preach. Her sermon challenged the women to fight for their homes. I felt that she was completely unaware of the situations that most women were living through. Some situations were very difficult to overcome; yet something inside of me stirred. I started to pray for my husband's spiritual restoration (my ex-husband at the time). I didn't ask the Lord to bring him home, but

to restore him as His son and for him to feel the
hunger to return to Him as his Heavenly Father. I
said, "Father, may this be for your glory and every
tongue be found a liar and you the only truth."

Several months later, my husband came to talk to me;
he never spoke to me for personal reasons. I told him
that without any spiritual reconciliation, there was
nothing to be said between us and every effort to
work on the relationship would be worthless. He
started to attend El Rey Jesus and after two or three
weeks, he surrendered his life to Jesus again. We
started dating again, but still living apart. I knew it
was important for us to be restored emotionally
before anything else happened. I remember that my
son, who was visiting us at the time, noticed that his
father and I were dating, and he said to me, "Mom, I
can't stand this, divorce was bad enough, but this
situation is even worse. Dad is never going to change.
He is not a church-going man." I answered him,
"Raulito, this is a testimony that will praise God and
if He has opened the door, I refuse to give Satan the
victory. The world will know that God is more
powerful and that when He opens doors, nobody can
close them. I am fighting the good fight and you will
be a witness to the victory." And this is exactly what
happened. Four months later and after talking to our
Pastor, we got remarried. We just celebrated our third
anniversary and we are actively serving in church.

Our family was completely restored! God had to deal with me first, dealing with the things that motivated me. I had to surrender my will completely to him and say, "Take my life and do with it what you will for your honor and glory."

God is faithful, wise and gives us second chances. He restores us. My husband and I enjoy a greater spiritual, emotional and physical union than before.

Newton and Gretchen Solomon

My wife and I were married in April of 1990. God blessed us with two beautiful children. We had a marriage, which throughout the years, started to disintegrate due to monotony and the webs that the enemy places around the family to destroy it. The collapse of our marriage happened in May 2000. At the time, we were living under the same roof, but totally separated from each other. The final blow came when my wife found me with another woman. This event marked my life to such an extent that I decided to end the marriage and I left home. We were divorced in September of that year.

The family was divided, the enemy happy, but God had other plans. Jesus had different plans for our lives. We were at such a low point in our lives that we had no choice but to look at God face to face. We knew that He had been with us through it all, but the blow of the divorce removed the veil from our eyes and finally opened our eyes to Him. We finally knew Him intimately. God created a miracle in our lives and it was sealed and guaranteed by Jesus. My wife was able to forgive my sin and welcomed me home again.

God has been so good to us. He allowed us to know Him at El Rey Jesus Church. For my wife and I, this has been an incredible blessing, to come to Jesus' feet through our Pastor and Apostle Guillermo Maldonado.

Jesus blended into our marriage and our Pastor united us again on April 13, 2002. Today, we are a close knit family and faithful to our Lord Jesus. My wife and I serve Him faithfully in the family ministry, helping to restore couples in the same way that Jesus did it with us.

God bless you! May this testimony help every couple who has overcome or who are going through a similar situation. All things are possible in Christ who is willing and able.

Armando Acosta and Yolai

On our wedding day, my wife and I questioned our motivation for getting married. We were unsure of our decision. We wondered if love was the reason we were getting married or if it was simply something that could benefit us mutually. I wondered if she still loved her ex-husband or not. On the other hand, there was a lot of pressure from the brothers (who had false and attended another church with my wife before we visited El Rey Jesus). This caused a lot of misunder-standings, not only in our relationship, but also with her children. The situation reached dangerous proportions, to the point of almost beating each other up. I made the decision at this time to leave home. I left feeling like I hated my wife and her children. She knew there was something that she needed to do. She made an appointment with the leaders in marriage counseling from El Rey Jesus Church. They gave her great advice. She was told to come and find me. Two weeks after our separation, she went looking for me. She asked for my forgiveness, not only for her mistakes, but also those of her children. She told me that she had read the Inner Healing and Deliverance book written by Pastor Guillermo Maldonado. She understood that the root of our problems was our lack of forgiveness for each other. Regardless of the humiliation that I had received from my wife, I listened to every word she had to say, but I was unmoved by her repentance. I told her that I hated her, and her children, and the last thing I wanted was to see her again. In her pain, she made the decision to fight for our marriage because she still loved me. This was enough to get her to pray on her knees and declare absolute fasting for three consecutive days a week. I was completely closed off, angry and trying to forget. My wife was fighting on her own, rebuking every spirit of divorce, separation, hate, unforgiveness and every other type of bondage that the Lord would show her. She didn't know where I was, but she still prayed for me, rebuking the stronghold that had come against our marriage and us. She also demanded of the enemy to loosen me from all unforgiveness and hate that was in me. And every spirit that was keeping me from understanding the truth had to leave. The prayers and battles were strong, but once more, my wife and I proved that there is nothing impossible for God.

I started to miss her and to worry about her. I realized that I still loved her. Two and a half months later, after our separation, I called her and told her to count on me for whatever needed to be done. She answered me very matter-of-fact, as if we had never been separated. She said that all of my belongings were in the same place, as if I had never left home and that I could return anytime I wanted. We started our relationship again by dating like boyfriend and girlfriend. We went for walks, shopping, talked on the phone, and before either of us knew it, we were together again. There was no condemnation from either side and all the rough edges in our relationship were gone. My wife and children took a firm grip on the Lord. They were attending church more than ever.

Their attitude towards me changed. Now we were enjoying our relationship like God's children. Watching them made me want to re-dedicate my life to Jesus. We joined the marriage counseling classes, which made a deep impact in our lives. We learned to differentiate our roles as husband and wife. We understood that our marriage is holy before God and that we have to respect and love our marriage covenant. After our reconciliation, we went through inner healing and deliverance. Today we serve in church together.

We are extremely thankful to the Lord for bringing us to our church and for our Pastors and leaders. We give the glory and the honor to God. Amen!

Gary and Mariela Bermudez

At the age of sixteen, I met a young man eighteen years old. We fell in love and shortly after I became pregnant. I left my parent's home and went to live with him. That is when all of my problems started. He was prone to violent rages; he was controlling and easily angered. I was a very naïve young woman, inexperienced, tender and very much in love. Regardless of his verbal, emotional and physical abuse, I stayed with him. We went through a lot of hard times; there was no respect for each other. Our first child was a daughter and later we had two sons. I found out that he had been unfaithful. I was tired of the situation and decided to break my relationship with God and from my husband. I had never experienced a personal relationship with Jesus; therefore, He was not Lord of my life. During this time, God started to do something new in my husband even though they were not obvious to me. It was then, that my husband started to pray for the restoration of our marriage; he didn't want it to dissolve. Bad character and all, he still loved me. He recognized that he had failed as a husband and that his abuse had caused many scars and painful wounds. He made the decision to follow Christ because he knew that He was the only one who could win this battle and restore our marriage. He continued to believe in God, even though the years were passing by and things were getting worse with me. During these difficult times, the Holy Spirit touched my heart and I was reconciled to my Lord, Jesus. I found peace and true love, the kind I had never experienced before. I felt a new life, birthed with hope, begin to grow inside of me. I really don't know how to explain it, but this was beautiful. We heard about inner healing and deliverance. We learned about the process and went through it. We were both very hurt and God delivered us from it all. I said to the Lord that if it was His will for me to return with my husband, then He needed to renew my love for him. I needed to fall in love with my husband all over again. He did it.

Where we thought there was no solution, and that everything was lost and finished, Jesus came in and brought restoration and answers to our lives and our children. If He can do it for us, then, my dear reader, He can do it for you too. It really doesn't matter what your situation is, perhaps it is worse than ours was, but if you allow God legal rights to work in your marriage, He will do it. We are extremely grateful and thankful for everything that He has done for us. Praise God!

Henry and Catalina Patiño

I remember that day very well; it was May 15, 1996 when Jesus, our Lord, finally knocked at my door after many failed attempts. This was an unforgettable day because it was the only option available to me before dying.

I knew that my time was running out during the last three months of my mundane life. My liver was totally destroyed, as was everything that was around me including my marriage, work and family.

I started drinking at the tender age of four. My wife and I came from dysfunctional homes. We had no idea what we were about to face the moment we were to say our marriage vows, especially because neither of us knew God. I had inherited the burden of the generational curse of alcoholism and experiencing the effects of the abuse I was inflicting upon my wife. My mother-in-law raised my wife by herself. She tried to teach her that she should never allow any man to hurt her. She understood what it feels like to be abused because she had been equally abused and mistreated. I, on the other hand, had a father who gave me, in excess, every thing I could ever need or want, materially speaking, but never anything spiritual. Four years into my relationship with my girlfriend, we made the decision to get married. The day I got married, I made the solid vow to never drink again. This was a vicious habit that was destroying my life little by little. Ironically, I drank more that day, than any other day, since it was the last day that I was going to drink. On our wedding day, when I stood before the judge, I was completely wasted. This was a terrible moment for my wife. Unfortunately, things did not improve after that. To prevent my wife from finding out that I was still drinking, I would walk my dog often. The doorman at my apartment building and our housekeeper hid my liquor. After my wife got home from the university, the only thing she received was verbal abuse and hard times; this was due to my drunkenness. I tried to hide the stench of liquor breath by sucking on hard candy and chewing on cloves to camouflage the bad breath, but she still noticed it. Little by little, she started to feel a deep sense of sadness. There was no respect left in our relationship. Sometime later I found myself in the hospital connected to different IV's and catheters for disintoxication of the excess of alcohol in my body. After that day, I stopped drinking for a week, but the desire for it was so strong that I started up again. My wife was so disillusioned in me that she looked for an escape to our problems by trusting in a friend from the university. She started to say, "If my husband continues drinking, then I will start drinking too." Three months before asking Jesus to come into my life, my body started to feel the damages caused by the alcohol abuse. My liver was completely non-functional and cirrhosis had set in; it was bleeding continually.

One day, I remember it was a Monday; my wife arrived from the university and found me completely drunk. That day I had drank eight bottles of wine in less than five hours. She was hitting me trying to wake me up to no avail. She made the decision that day to pack her bags and leave home. She moved in with her mother. Before she left, the only thing I could think to say was, "You can go, but the dog and the car stay with me."

The next day, May 15th, the Lord knocked on my door through a Colombian Christian actress who had a primetime show. She arrived at my office to propose a commercial exchange. That was the most important

day of my life; radical changes started to happen.
Fifteen days after this visit, my wife returned home.
She had understood that there was a divine plan and
purpose for our lives. We had no idea where to go
from there. For five months, we attended a church in
Colombia where we were sent to Miami to begin a
personal discipleship. We spent two and a half years
in a church that thought we were ready to be sent into
ministry. When we finished our Biblical studies, the
pastor, who was our mentor, tells us his plans to send
us to Guatemala to help open a mission in Lago
Atitlan. We humbly accepted. We felt uneasy about
the move, but I guess we believed we were ready for
it, but God's plans are perfect and He knew we were
not ready. Since the desire of our hearts was to serve
Him, He changed the church we were in. Suddenly,
my wife and I decided to go our separate ways and
devote our time to the study of the Word, to seek God
and try to understand God's plan for our lives.
Everywhere we went and everyone who talked to us
mentioned El Rey Jesus Church. Since our first visit to
the church, we realized that we had a lot to learn.
Although our marriage had improved, we had no
Biblical foundation to build a family. We didn't
understand the needs or requirements of a man or
woman. We didn't have to go through counseling to
understand the areas in our lives that were failing,
personally and as a couple. One month after that first
visit at El Rey Jesus, Pastor Maldonado preached one

entire series on the family. Everyday after that, each teaching became rhema in our lives. We experienced hard times in the church, which God used to mature us in the areas we needed to improve in. I dare to say that since that day that the pastor taught on the family, I started to know and understand the woman that God had given me. It is important to understand that knowing Jesus is not enough to make things right again. This is the first step. Next, is the process of preparation for marriage, which includes getting rid of everything we drag from our parents and ancestors; the things that we have to change. We need to be ministered in inner healing and deliverance. Furthermore, we need to learn God's design for the family. I remember talking to an older couple. We were counseling them when they said, *"You are not going to teach me about marriage, I can teach you because I have been married five times."*

It is very important to have the desire to change. I remember the day that I said to Jesus, even before I invited Him to come into my heart that I knew that He was no longer hanging on the cross. I asked Him to give me an exemplary marriage.

Marriage is a sacred institution, but we have to understand how two very different people, with different needs, feelings and emotions can come together and compliment each other.

Respect and admiration are evident in our marriage, and above all, complete trust in the Lord, who is a vital part of our existence. We are absolutely sure that we are building our marriage according to God's specifications. Allow me to tell you, my dear reader, that there is still time for change. Make the decision to change today! Marriage is a sacred institution established by God. Divorce is Satan's plan to destroy what God has instituted. Jesus is being glorified more and more today because of it. *"27But God has chosen the foolish things of the world to put to shame the wise." 1 Corinthians 1.27*

We are convinced that the information that you just read will change the lives of people who feel secure in their marriage, but the revelation imparted by the Holy Spirit through the pages of this book will also dramatically change your lives and take you to new levels in Him.

"18And the LORD God said, "It is not good that man should be alone; I will make him a helper comparable to him." Genesis 2.18

God bless you!

Bibliography

Biblia de Estudio Arco Iris. Version Reina-Valera, Revision 1960, Biblical Text copyright© 1960, Sociedades Bíblicas in Latin America, Nashville, Tennessee, ISBN: 1-55819-555-6.

Biblia Plenitud. 1960 Reina-Valera Revision, ISBN: 089922279X, Caribe Editorial, Miami, Florida.

Diccionario Español a Inglés, Inglés a Español. Larousse Editorial S.A., impreso en Dinamarca, Núm. 81, México, ISBN: 2-03-420200-7, ISBN: 70-607-371-X, 1993.

El Pequeño Larousse Ilustrado. 2002 Spes Editorial, S.L. Barcelona; Ediciones Larousse, S.A. de C.V. México, D.F., ISBN: 970-22-0020-2.

Expanded Edition the Amplified Bible. Zondervan Bible Publishers. ISBN: 0-31095168-2, 1987 – lockman foundation USA.

Reina-Valera 1995 - Edición de Estudio, USA: Sociedades Bíblicas Unidas) 1998.

Strong James, LL.D, S.T.D., *Concordancia Strong Exhaustiva de la Biblia*, Caribe Editorial, Inc., Thomas

Nelson, Inc., Publishers, Nashville, TN - Miami, FL, EE.UU., 2002. ISBN: 0-89922-382-6.

The New American Standard Version. Zordervan Publishing Company, ISBN: 0310903335, pages 255-266.
The Tormont Webster's Illustrated Encyclopedic Dictionary. ©1990 Tormont Publications. Pages 255-266.

Vine, W.E. *Diccionario Expositivo de las Palabras del Antiguo Testamento y Nuevo Testamento*. Caribe Editorial, Inc./División Thomas Nelson, Inc., Nashville, TN, ISBN: 0-89922-495-4, 1999.

Ward, Lock A. *Nuevo Diccionario de la Biblia*. Unilit Editorial: Miami, Florida, ISBN: 0-7899-0217-6, 1999.

OUR VISION

PUBLICATIONS

The objective of our mission is to spiritually feed God's people through preaching and teaching and to take the Word of God everywhere it is needed.

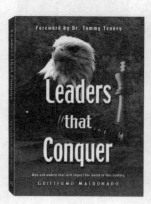

LEADERS THAT CONQUER

Guillermo Maldonado
ISBN: 1-59272-023-4 *

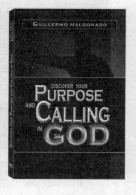

DISCOVER YOUR PURPOSE AND CALLING IN GOD

Guillermo Maldonado
ISBN: 1-59272-019-6

FORGIVENESS

Guillermo Maldonado
ISBN: 188392717-X *

THE FAMILY

Guillermo Maldonado
ISBN: 1-59272-024-2

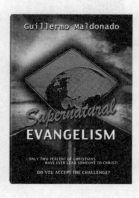

SUPERMATURAL EVANGELISM

Guillermo Maldonado
ISBN: 159272013-7

BIBLICAL FOUNDATIONS FOR A NEW BELIEVER

Guillermo Maldonado
ISBN: 1-59272-005-6

* Books available also in Spanish and French.

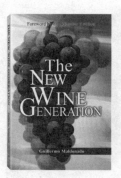
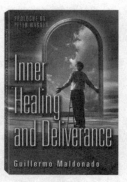
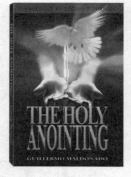